Plays By
Y York

Broadway Play Publishing Inc
New York
BroadwayPlayPub.com

Plays By Y York

Cover photo: Tom Chargin

First printing: June 2000
I S B N: 978-0-88145-177-1

Book design: Marie Donovan
Copy editing: Michele Travis
Typeface: Palatino

CONTENTS

ABOUT THE AUTHOR

Y York is a 1994 graduate of New Dramatists and recipient of N D's Joe Callaway Award. Y's plays have received support from the King County, Seattle Arts Commissions, and Artists' Trust. She received a 1997 Berrilla Kerr Playwriting Award and is a member of The Dramatists' Guild.
In addition to writing plays, Y was an occasional writer for *Little Bear,* an animated character on the Nick Jr. channel, and for Videodiscovery, a producer of interactive media. Her plays are produced with something approaching regularity at adult and family theatres across the country. Family plays include: AFTERNOON OF THE ELVES; THE GARDEN OF RIKKI TIKKI TAVI; ACCIDENTAL FRIENDS; THE PORTRAIT THE WIND THE CHAIR; FROG AND TOAD (FOREVER); THE WITCH OF BLACKBIRD POND; THE LAST PAVING STONE, and MASK OF THE UNICORN WARRIOR. Adult plays include: AMERICAN 60S IN THREE AX; THE BOTTOM OF THE NINTH; IT COMES AROUND; KRISIT; LIFE GAP; RAIN. SOME FISH. NO ELEPHANTS. (also published by Broadway Play Publishing Inc); THE PRINCESS INSIDE VERSUS THE NEW DARK CLARITY; and TOAST AND JAM. Y lives with Mark Lutwak, to whom most things are dedicated.

THE SECRET WIFE

ACKNOWLEDGMENTS

For support with the development of THE SECRET WIFE, thanks to New Dramatists; The Playwrights' Theater of New Jersey; Arena Stage in DC; ASK Theater Projects in L A; and The Seattle Arts Commission.

die Rechtfertigung
und
die Verzeihung

CHARACTERS & SETTING

SYLVIA: *thirties, American, wife of* NOEL
NOEL: *thirties, American*
HARRY: *forties, American*
JEREMY: *fifties, American*
MARY: *fifties, American,* JEREMY*'s wife*
LILA: *forties, American,* HARRY*'s wife*
FRAU RICHTER: *twenties. German landlady, played by a young male actor of African descent. This character is a woman; the actor is in drag, the character isn't. Young, nosy, nationalistic.*

MIKHAIL: *forties, Soviet, played by the actor who plays* HARRY
VARYA: *forties, Soviet, played by the actor who plays* LILA
IVAN: *thirties, Soviet, played by the actor who plays* NOEL
KING TUT: *3,520s, Egyptian, played by the actor who plays* FRAU RICHTER. *Perky, sexy, young, astonishingly contemporary.*

All of the above characters are played by seven actors.

Note: Although these humans are plagued with many problems, as are we all, including insecurity and skepticism, none of them are afflicted with rising intonations at the end of sentences that do not have question marks. Also, nobody smokes.

The action of the play is continuous—there are no blackouts between scenes. An over-sized telephone is always present.

Time and place: West Germany, 1972

DISCLAIMER: This is a play.

ACT ONE

Scene One

(The American office. SYLVIA, NOEL, *and* HARRY *demonstrating with a purse)*

HARRY: You hold it like this, see, over the *shoulder*, it's a *shoulder* bag, right? The lens is down here, see?

SYLVIA: And how do I focus?

HARRY: Focus, no. You can't be holding your purse up to your face, now, can ya? That doesn't look natural, and the whole idea is to look natural, to fade away, to be invisible.

SYLVIA: *(Nodding)* Invisible.

HARRY: Not too pretty, not too ugly—you know, your hair...

SYLVIA: My hair...?

HARRY: Yeah, you should think about a haircut.

SYLVIA: But I never cut—?

HARRY: Or up, wear it up; one of those up-do's. Something a little less big. Now, you got the hang of the camera?

SYLVIA: Um, the lens is—*(Where exactly?)*

HARRY: *(Demonstrating* again*)* Just sort of aim it and click, aim and click, click, click, click—walk away—look in shop windows—tisk at prices, like that. You'll blend in—"I am the shopping German-hausfrau, filling my basket and showing my disdain," aim, click, tisk. Here. *(Hands her purse, exiting)* I got some recording equipment I wanna show you—

*(*HARRY *exits.* SYLVIA *struggles with purse.)*

SYLVIA: Oy—

NOEL: Hon, don't say "oy."

SYLVIA: No, this is a truly oy situation.

NOEL: If you want to make friends with some German, you don't want him to know you're Jewish.

SYLVIA: There's nobody German here.

NOEL: You want to get in the habit.

SYLVIA: Noel, you never said I had to help.

NOEL: ...They don't want to waste the language training.

SYLVIA: I'm not good with cameras. It takes me hours to focus.

NOEL: You don't have to focus. Like Harry said, aim and click. That's it.

SYLVIA: What about my hair?

NOEL: Invisible. The word of the hour is invisible. *(Playful)* Hey, I'll still love you without your hair.

*(*HARRY *reenters.)*

HARRY: *(Disbelief)* You made a request for absentee ballots?

SYLVIA: Oh yes, yes I did.

HARRY: Why waste the paper? Nixon's a shoe-in.

NOEL: I hear he's worried.

HARRY: He's not worried.

NOEL: Then what about the break-in?

HARRY: That is *nothing*. That is going to be nothing.

SYLVIA: I always vote. Even though they never win.

HARRY: Sixty-eight? Nixon.

NOEL: *(To cover)* She was too young in '68.

SYLVIA: I don't vote Republican.

NOEL: *(To cover)* Isn't she cute?

HARRY: Yeah, it usually doesn't make any difference, but McGovern—no thank you...hey, just a—*(Whisper) Jeremy* has absolutely no sense of humor about politics. Okay! So. *(Showing device)* Look at this *little guy*. Amazing.

NOEL: Oh, yeah—we used those little guys in Nam.

HARRY: Where they were very handy. So—you're at a restaurant, you go to the bathroom, you leave your bag on the table—

SYLVIA: *(Nodding)* The one with the camera.

HARRY: No. ...*Not* the one with the camera, you never leave that. *Another* one, another *time*, a time when you take a real bag, a real purse. You leave your real purse on the table with the little guy inside recording their conversation.

SYLVIA: I can't go to the bathroom without my bag. It has all my stuff.

HARRY: You don't *need* your stuff. Becaaause. You don't really *go* to the bathroom. I mean you *do* go to the bathroom but you don't have to.

SYLVIA: *(Nodding)* It's a false alarm.

HARRY: You're going to the bathroom in order to leave your *bag behind*. So your friends have a chance to *talk*. Really talk. What they say when you're gone is the only thing that counts. What they say while you're *there* is cheese.

SYLVIA: Who are these people?

HARRY: Who do you think? You got jet lag or something?

SYLVIA: Maybe I *do*.

HARRY: We gotta be top fit, girl. This ain't America. We got Communists and Fascists and religious fanatics—they don't stay in their own country any more.

SYLVIA: ...I had...*language training*—guten tag mein Herr.

HARRY: Language training be damned. You had two years next to the man.

SYLVIA: What man—*(Are you talking about?)*

NOEL: *(Interrupts)* Harry, Harry, Harry. Slow down. We just got here. I'm tired, Sylvia's tired.

HARRY: The enemy never sleeps.

NOEL: Could you ...excuse us for a minute? *(Pause)* Come on, give us a minute, Harry.

HARRY: ...Oh, brother. *(Exits)*

SYLVIA: Am I supposed to *hear* this?

NOEL: Hon, hush.

SYLVIA: Hush?! Don't tell me to—

NOEL: Hon, Hon, it's a little...mix up.

SYLVIA: It feels like a *big* mix up.

NOEL: It's about my other Silvia. ...Silvia with an "*I*" instead of a "*Y*"?

SYLVIA: *(Mad)* What *about* your Silvia with an "*I*" instead of a "*Y*"?

NOEL: They think you're her.

SYLVIA: They think I'm the *spying* Silvia?

NOEL: Hon, don't say spying.

SYLVIA: I'm not supposed to get hidden camera training?

NOEL: Wives get language training. Not surveillance training.

SYLVIA: Well, let's *tell* them.

NOEL: Hon, Hon, Hon. That's the last thing you do; this is the government. If somebody makes a mistake and you *tell* them, it's no longer a *mistake*, it's a *catastrophe* and it makes them look bad and they take it out on you. Harry's our support. We don't want him mad at us, not even a little bit.

SYLVIA: What if somebody finds out?

NOEL: They won't. They might if you had a desk or a paycheck, but you don't, so it's fine. *(Hand in pocket)* Oh. Sylvia—I—

SYLVIA: No. Don't spring something else on me, Noel.

NOEL: No, this is good.

SYLVIA: You don't say my name when it's good.

NOEL: *(Hands pill bottle to her)* Doc gave me these pills for your allergy. So you can drink wine and beer.

SYLVIA: I don't drink wine and beer.

NOEL: Hon, in Germany *everybody* drinks wine and beer; if you don't, you will not be invisible.

Scene Two

*(*SYLVIA *in her apartment. She picks up the over-large phone.)*

SYLVIA: *(To* NOEL, *off)* I'm going to try to call home.

(She dials many numbers. A knock on the door.)

SYLVIA: Noel, can you—? Oh, never mind.

(Hangs up. Enter FRAU RICHTER *with a magazine. They speak German.)*

FRAU: Pardon, meine Frau. Here ist dein magazine.

SYLVIA: Oh, danke, Frau Richter, that fast was, I just yesterday called—

FRAU: Ja, well, du bist in Germany, now.

SYLVIA: I know. Where the trains on schedule run.

FRAU: I inside it peeked. Look. Harry Bellafonte.

SYLVIA: Oh. He a great singer is.

FRAU: Ja. Part German.

SYLVIA: *(Looking inside)* Does it that say?

FRAU: Nein, but true is. I distantly related to him am.

SYLVIA: He doesn't German look.

FRAU: *(Insulted)* You can't always by looking tell.

SYLVIA: Will he be by coming?

FRAU: Nein. ...May I, for a moment, frank be?

SYLVIA: Sure. What's up?

FRAU: There was eine grosse shrei aus your bedroom in der nacht.

SYLVIA: ...Last nacht?

FRAU: Jawol.

SYLVIA: Oh. I really sorry am. We'll try to quiet be. Is *your* bedroom...right above *our* bedroom, or something?

FRAU: Ja. Unbelievably lout was. Eine shrei exactly like ein stereo elefanten fluken zounden blasten.

SYLVIA: I assure you, we do *not*—no stereo blasten.

FRAU: Ja, gut. May I frank be once again?

SYLVIA: Sure! Why not?

FRAU: You must in der boutique ge-shoppen.

SYLVIA: I don't the fancy stores like.

FRAU: Nein. Pretty frau like you, *(Pats* SYLVIA*'s cheek) must* in der boutique ge-shoppen. You do not die Turkish guestworkers, or die Arabish guestworkers, or die Greekish guestworkers want to encounter. Die guestworkers unbelievably schmutzig are. *(Tisks)*

SYLVIA: ...Really?

FRAU: Ja. They dirty filthy unwashed scum are. *(Tisks)*

SYLVIA: I never would have known.

FRAU: Ja. *(Very intimate)* Und they everywhere are. Guestworkers eine mistake das come back to haunt us will. Die Arabish people, they can't Deutsche sprechen, und their kinder to school right next to our kinder go.

SYLVIA: Well, that seems—*(Perfectly reasonable to me.)*

FRAU: They tell us, we must guestworkers for das work force haben, but meanwhile we unemployment haben. Does that even sense make?

SYLVIA: Not to me, but—

FRAU: I wanted you about das stores to know. Aufwiedersehen.

*(*FRAU RICHTER *kisses her on the cheek and exits tisking.)*

SYLVIA: Wiedersehen. Oh, thank you so much. Click aim tisk. Click aim tisk.

(Enter NOEL.*)*

NOEL: What did Frau Richter want?

SYLVIA: She wanted to give me a lesson in German-hausfrau-disdain. Click aim tisk.

NOEL: No, Hon, not click aim tisk. Aim click tisk.

SYLVIA: She doesn't want me to get soiled by the filthy Arab guestworkers.

NOEL: Whoa. She's not exactly a native herself.

SYLVIA: She was *born* here, Noel.

NOEL: That doesn't make her a native German.

SYLVIA: Well she's *half* a native German, and that half wants us to stop aiming our stereo speakers at the ceiling.

NOEL: What stereo speakers—?

SYLVIA: The ones blasting elephant mating calls.

NOEL: Oh. *(Chuckle)* Sorry.

SYLVIA: Elefanten flucken zounden blasten.

NOEL: *(Manly man)* Come here, my little elefanten. *(An embrace)* I suddenly sense another fluken zounden erupten.

SYLVIA: *(Nuzzling)* Something has come over you in Germany.

NOEL: Is this a complaint?

SYLVIA: No no. Just an observation. You're a new man in Germany. *(Getting turned on)* Oh...Noel...

NOEL: I love it when you say my name. It's so sexy.

SYLVIA: Is that why...?

NOEL: ...Why what?

SYLVIA: Last night—um—

NOEL: Last night was great.

SYLVIA: Oh it *was*...we almost got there.

NOEL: What are you talking "almost?" We got there.

SYLVIA: Not all of us got there.

NOEL: Hey, don't worry. You'll get the hang of it.

SYLVIA: Yeah, but maybe you could—

NOEL: Me? Hon. This isn't about *me.* Is that *Der Spiegel*?

SYLVIA: Can we stay on the subject please?

NOEL: I just need to check—oh, too bad, there it is.

SYLVIA: What?

NOEL: The break-in. At least it isn't on the cover.

SYLVIA: It was on the *front page* of the Post.

NOEL: The *Post* only matters in D C. The world doesn't notice unless it's in *Der Spiegel* or *The Times.*

Scene Three

*(*JEREMY *and* MARY *in their apartment with* SYLVIA *and* NOEL, *after dinner.)*

JEREMY: It's economic *mumbo jumbo* if it doesn't have a real world basis.

SYLVIA: Supply and demand.

JEREMY: Exactly.

SYLVIA: Brand loyalty.

JEREMY: Well, no. Supply and demand, yes. But brand loyalty is a *pseudo* economic reality.

SYLVIA: But, Jeremy, brand loyalty has an effect—*(on the economy)*

MARY: I don't think it's pseudo.

NOEL: Brands are just so much advertising.

SYLVIA: But so is demand, Noel. If we're talking economic realities here. T V! You demand it because you see it a thousand times on T V. Demand *is* demand, it isn't *need.*

MARY: *(Agrees)* If I'm shopping for Camay, Brand X will not do.

SYLVIA: You *demand* it.

MARY: Because of my brand loyalty.

NOEL: You have to look at the life-and-death issues, Mary.

MARY: I'll die if I don't get the right soap.

SYLVIA: *(Agrees)* Because of advertising.

NOEL: Like food and water.

JEREMY: And money.

NOEL: You have to look at how market forces function in starving nations.

JEREMY: The dog-eat-dog desperation of human beings starving to death.

SYLVIA: Let's just send them food.

JEREMY: You diminish the man when you send him food. Let him work for it to enhance his own self-worth.

NOEL: *(Toasts)* Hear, hear.

JEREMY: And what's wrong with being practical? Looking after our *own* interests while we're letting our starving friend earn a dollar. *(Rhetorical)* How can he help us? He doesn't have anything we want to buy; we certainly don't want him becoming part of our work force.

SYLVIA: *(Sincere)* Is he Arab?

NOEL: Hon, please—

JEREMY: Let's put him to work *there;* start an on-site industry in his own homeland.

NOEL: Using local resources.

JEREMY: Of which there aren't any or he wouldn't need our help. All this guy's got is space. Big open barren space, growing nothing and fostering nothing. Let's put it to use. Let them store our radioactive waste.

NOEL: *(Nodding)* The article in *The American Speculator—*

JEREMY: Everything has some inherent value. Starving countries are suddenly no longer a liability.

SYLVIA: Nobody's going to buy our radioactivity, Jeremy.

JEREMY: They don't *buy* it, Sylvia. We ship it to them and *pay them* to take it. It provides a sudden infusion of hard cash to a country with no food, no medicine, and a life expectancy of twenty-nine.

SYLVIA: They won't do it.

JEREMY: Yes. They will. ...Now, don't be short sighted, Sylvia. Radioactivity is dangerous over *extended* exposure. It takes *years.* By the time these people have lived that long, they're dead anyway.

(Brief pause)

MARY: How are you settling in, Dear?

SYLVIA: Okay. Your place is so nice.

NOEL: Nice? It's downright opulent.

MARY: Well, it takes a while; we've been here for years.

SYLVIA: We won't be here that long.

MARY: Really? Jeremy said...

JEREMY: *(To* NOEL*)* I wouldn't let *that* get around.

NOEL: *(To* SYLVIA*)* Well, we don't *know* that, Hon.

SYLVIA: That's not what you *said—*

JEREMY: It takes at least five years to get things going, Noel. If you leave after one or two tours, what's going to happen to your *people*? Are you going to turn your people over to somebody they don't know?

SYLVIA: *(To* NOEL*) Two* years.

MARY: That's what *I* thought. *One* tour, then back to D C. But two years later, there are a hundred little *unfinished* projects. Four years later, there are three or four important people *in place.*

(Brief pause)

JEREMY: Are you two going to get down to Munich? For the Olympics?

NOEL: I can't take the time.

JEREMY: But it's the *Olympics,* boy. A chance for Americans to thrash the competition. Sylvia will love it. And you have to see the King Tut exhibit.

SYLVIA: *(Frightened)* No no, we don't want to see that.

NOEL: Hon—

SYLVIA: There's a curse, a terrible curse—

NOEL: Hon, that's superstition.

SYLVIA: Why risk it? There were horrible deaths.

JEREMY: It's a lovely show. Gold jewelry and whatnot.

SYLVIA: Many deaths. Many. Anybody who went in the tomb, anybody who touched his mummy. I know what I'm talking about. I studied the Egyptians.

JEREMY: Then you'll want to see the exhibit. *(Disdain)* My stars. Take the time, Noel. Besides, it won't really be a vacation, if you know what I mean.

(Brief pause)

MARY: More wine?

SYLVIA: No thanks.

NOEL: I will, thank you. Nice Bordeaux.

JEREMY: Burgundy, actually.

NOEL: Oh. It's dark for a burgundy.

JEREMY: No, it's an excellent burgundy.

NOEL: Maybe the bottle was mis-labeled.

JEREMY: Mis—I got it at auction!

NOEL: It happens; even the best chateaus.

MARY: *(To* JEREMY*)* The glass is tinted, dear.

JEREMY: For *red wine*?! *(He pours the wine into a clear glass.)*

SYLVIA: They're very pretty.

MARY: Thank you.

JEREMY: You can't see the color, the legs.

NOEL: You gotta see the legs.

JEREMY: The first sign of a wine's ancestry.

NOEL: And to check for poison. *(Chuckle)* Not that I was looking for that tonight. *Now* I see. Beautiful.

JEREMY: I should hope so. It's a '55. That was *the* year for Burgundy. Limited stock.

NOEL: Superb. And Mary, that was a delicious meal. I love sweetbreads.

JEREMY: Yes, the brains of the beast.

NOEL: Oh, my mistake. I thought they were sweetbreads.

JEREMY: Sweetbreads *are* brains.

MARY: Dear—

NOEL: Not officially, I don't think.

JEREMY: Yes, that's what you get when you order them.

NOEL: Only if the restaurant is cheating. Sweetbreads are the pancreas and the whatnot glands.

JEREMY: Brains.

NOEL: Maybe we should look it up.

JEREMY: Yes, I think we should.

(A dictionary. They look it up.)

NOEL: Glands.

SYLVIA: *(Pointedly)* Maybe it's different in Europe, Noel.

JEREMY: Maybe it is. So, cigar?

NOEL: I don't—

JEREMY: They're Havannas.

NOEL: *(Taking one)* In that case—

MARY: You men take your stinky cigars to the den, Jeremy.

JEREMY: All right, Mary. Shall we?

NOEL: By all means.

*(*JEREMY *and* NOEL *exit.)*

MARY: I don't know what gets into them. I mean who cares, right? As long as it's not going to poison us, who cares which part of the beast it is?

SYLVIA: Maybe the beast.

MARY: Not by the time it's parts. Does Noel smoke?

SYLVIA: I've never seen him smoke.

MARY: Good. I hate it when Jeremy actually lights them. So. Have you met everybody?

SYLVIA: Harry. Frau Richter our landlady.

MARY: I should have called sooner.

SYLVIA: That's okay; I've been busy. I have to write a dissertation, and before I can do that I have to pick a *topic.* I almost did King Tut— *(Gasp, brief pause)* ...whoa, I get the creeps just saying his name.

MARY: I beg your pardon?

SYLVIA: His head was all smashed in. They unwrapped the tape on his dried-up little mummy, and there was this crushed little skull. Somebody had thwacked him.

MARY: Thwacked?

SYLVIA: Yeah, he never knew what hit him. Ka-pow-ee. He was cute, too, but why open a can of worms when there might be a bomb inside?

MARY: *(Brief pause)* What *is* your field?

SYLVIA: History. I'm a history person.

MARY: You should pick some history from here.

SYLVIA: None of it *looks* like history; it all looks like modern America.

MARY: Well, Americans rebuilt it. More wine, Dear?

SYLVIA: *(Taking a pill)* Oh, sure, why not.

MARY: Are you and Noel planning on starting your family soon?

SYLVIA: I don't want children.

MARY: Does Noel know?

SYLVIA: Yes, of course. I'm getting a degree.

MARY: Oh, yes. I didn't know that meant no kids.

SYLVIA: Don't look so sad.

MARY: You should meet the other wives. Find out how we cope.

SYLVIA: I've never been very good with...um....

MARY: ...Wives?

SYLVIA: Yeah.

MARY: That's because you weren't one—now that you *are* one you'll *get* good. You need girlfriends when you fight.

SYLVIA: We don't fight.

MARY: Yes, but when you do, you need girlfriends, and it's better to look for them in-house. Did you meet Harry's wife?

SYLVIA: No.

MARY: Lila is quite lively. You might like her; of course, you also might not. When the kids went to college, all I had were my friends.

SYLVIA: You had Jeremy.

(MARY *snorts.* NOEL *reenters.)*

NOEL: Hon, no hair cut. Not yet.

Scene Four

*(*MARY *in her apartment with* SYLVIA *and* LILA*)*

LILA: Harry and I were a great team; he was gadgets, gizmos, and traps; I was people. I focused on personalities.

MARY: Lila was the magnet.

LILA: Harry snagged more guys who came over to talk to me. I was a psychic.

SYLVIA: Reading palms? And like that?

LILA: Palms and Tarot cards. Boy, people love that junk. Me, me, me. Tell me more about me.

SYLVIA: But what would you *say*?

LILA: I'd skim the file beforehand to find *the* thing to hook the guy. It was always the same, the career or sex.

SYLVIA: It sounds like the perfect come-on.

LILA: *(Defensive)* It wasn't totally fake. I mean, it started out as a come-on, but after a while I got really good at it.

MARY: Everybody said you were terrific.

SYLVIA: Why did you quit?

LILA: *(Sarcasm)* For the excitement of motherhood.

MARY: You know you love motherhood.

LILA: It's tough to go from being one of the guys to being one of the guy's wives. Females, I'm telling ya, we're good at this.

MARY: We're more perceptive.

LILA: Our tolerance for the grotesque is greater.

MARY: From babies.

LILA: From diapers. Harry gets so upset about stuff, but as soon as he tells it to me, he's okay.

MARY: Like confession.

LILA: Yeah. I take all them filthy secrets down to the wash and bleach 'em clean. *I* never have nightmares.

SYLVIA: Women are stronger.

LILA: More ruthless.

SYLVIA: No, I don't think so.

LILA: Unless you touch our soft spots. Touch our soft spots, we get all giddy, start dropping our security secrets like bread crumbs. ...What is this yummy thing?

MARY: Hot-buttered rum.

LILA: Oh, no, we stopped butter.

MARY: You can't stop butter in Germany.

LILA: For real, stopped.

MARY: I'll get the wine.

LILA: The doctor says we should quit red meat, too.

MARY: I don't think we have that problem.

LILA: I have it very bad.

MARY: My. Wine, Dear?

SYLVIA: Oh. *(Taking a pill)* Okay.

LILA: The worst the doctor's ever seen in a living person. It's from eating butter on sausage in the fashion of the host country.

MARY: My doctor says food doesn't make any difference to health.

LILA: When you're dead he'll think so.

MARY: No. He doesn't believe it. He thinks it's a conspiracy.

LILA: God, Mary, don't go to those *company* guys; go to a German doctor.

MARY: They cost an arm and a leg.

LILA: It's bad enough without going to a company *doctor.* A person has to find *some* privacy.

MARY: Certainly no privacy at home.

LILA: You're telling me. Harry is always competing for some bedroom academy award.

*(*MARY *and* LILA *laugh.)*

MARY: How nice for you, Dear.

LILA: Oh, I'm so sick of it.

SYLVIA: What?

LILA: God forbid the enemy thinks he can't satisfy his wife. We never would have figured it out, except I bragged about Harry's "attentiveness" to the other wives. Then some of us compared notes. It's the idea of a bugged apartment. It turns them all into Casanova.

MARY: Almost all.

SYLVIA: ...You mean—? Oh—

LILA: She's noticed.

*(*MARY *and* LILA *laugh.)*

SYLVIA: Oh, no. It isn't that.

LILA: *(Sarcasm)* Oh no, it couldn't be that.

MARY: They are newlyweds, after all.

LILA: Let me see the ring.

*(*SYLVIA *displays rings.)*

LILA: Very nice. Very just-like-mine.

SYLVIA: I love it, of course, but I wanted something a little unique.

LILA: No no. No deviations from the norm.

MARY: Diamonds were out of fashion when we got engaged.

LILA: I don't remember diamonds ever being out of fashion.

MARY: Yes, there was some nasty conspiracy rumor.... A Jewish conspiracy to make Christians buy diamond rings.

LILA: I never heard that one.

SYLVIA: *(Very uncomfortable)* ...The ring tradition is *Roman. Ancient* Roman. *(She pours herself more wine.)*

MARY: Maybe, but the diamond tradition is much more recent and much more Jewish.

LILA: Remember being a newlywed, Mary? The hopes, the dreams.

MARY: Vaguely.

LILA: The company claims another marriage.

SYLVIA: ...Not my one. The company won't claim my one.

LILA: Sure, honey. Did you have The Big Wedding?

SYLVIA: Yes, Noel's mother insisted.

MARY: Oh, dear, has your mother passed away?

SYLVIA: Um, no. My mother, she wasn't, um—

LILA: Wasn't into the union, huh?

SYLVIA: Not exactly.

MARY: Why ever not? Noel's a catch.

SYLVIA: He's not...he's not—

LILA: She'll come around.

MARY: You never let anybody finish a sentence.

LILA: Pardon meeee! *(To SYLVIA)* Go ahead.

SYLVIA: ...No. I'm done.

MARY: You should wait for the punctuation at the end of the sentence, Lila, before you speak.

LILA: Pardon me Period. Is that one of Jeremy's edicts Question Mark?

MARY: Jeremy doesn't give me edicts. He doesn't talk to me at all.

LILA: Yeah? Does he think you're a security risk?

MARY: I'm not as interesting as a security risk.

LILA: It gets harder and harder to hold their attention.

MARY: It gets impossible.

LILA: *(To SYLVIA)* Not for newlyweds, of course, for whom it is all so very...new. I wouldn't go back, though.

MARY: I would.

LILA: Re-live all that fumbling, unsatisfying sex? No thanks.

SYLVIA: We don't...we don't fumble.

LILA: Right. *(Laughs)* Don't worry, Dear. It'll get better.

MARY: Or go away entirely.

LILA: You have to stay inventive. ...Do you remember the Sawyers?

MARY: How could I possible forget the Sawyers?

LILA: Right. Connie Sawyer was always on me and Harry to help save their marriage.

MARY: Connie seemed very inventive.

LILA: Yeah, she went on and on about how we should all take a bath together.

MARY: To save the marriage?

LILA: Well, not for hygiene.

MARY: You didn't take a bath, did you?

LILA: We did. It was very tight. Me and Harry didn't even guess what they wanted until they flat-out asked. We thought it was an innocent little bath.

SYLVIA: Did it work?

LILA: Did what work?

SYLVIA: Did it save their marriage?

LILA: I guess it did. They're still married. So are we, come to think of it.

SYLVIA: ...This is reminding me of something.

LILA: What?

SYLVIA: Something else. Something from before... *(Realizes)* Women's Consciousness Raising Group.

MARY: I read about that.

LILA: Never heard of it.

SYLVIA: Yeah, I went to one. Women get together. Talk. Cheer each other up. *(Pours wine)* Somebody said how her husband wasn't interested anymore. Everybody chimed in with ideas.

LILA: Yes? Bathing with the neighbors?

SYLVIA: No. *(Tries to remember)* ...You touch him.

LILA: *(Laughs)* Where?!

SYLVIA: Yeah. You reach out your arm. Sneak it across the sheet to his side of the mattress. Cool fingers gently stroke hot, broad, male, back.

MARY: I haven't let my hands wander into his portion of the mattress in years. He'll jump up and yell at me.

LILA: It's worth a try. Maybe it won't be his back. Maybe you'll stretch your investigating fingers across the sheet and find...a front!

MARY: I could never.

SYLVIA: That's it. That's what you're supposed to do. Stroke his front.

MARY: No, it could make things much worse. If I go poking around in the sheet, it will make him very quiet.

LILA: Have *you* tried it?

SYLVIA: Nope.

LILA: Well, what do *you* do?

SYLVIA: *(Embarrassed)* —I don't know.

LILA: Look at all that facial pinkness. She's hiding a something, a secret method; she's holding out.

MARY: They're newlyweds, Lila.

LILA: No, she's a holdout, Mary! She has a trick! A secret trick. *(Makes it up.)* I'll bet she lies in bed waiting for it and when nothing happens, she wiggles; she wiggles her behind against his behind.

(SYLVIA giggles.)

LILA: *(Continued)* Look, it's true!

SYLVIA: No!

LILA: How about wiggling, Mary?

MARY: No. It's too dangerous.

LILA: What are you going to do for fun?

MARY: Same as always. Shopping.

SYLVIA: Let's go shopping. *(To MARY)* I saw something that will look great on you.

Scene Five

(The American office. JEREMY and HARRY, with a file.)

JEREMY: You can't have it.

HARRY: It's a directive. Somebody's got to take it. Let me have a shot.

JEREMY: No. You alone—his antenna will be up. I'm giving it to Noel and Sylvia.

HARRY: What am I, cheese all of a sudden?

(Enter NOEL with a file.)

NOEL: Oh, sorry.

JEREMY: No, no. Come in. We were just talking about you.

NOEL: We got a call. The Syrians are beefing up security.

JEREMY: All right. Warn the Embassy.

HARRY: *(Miffed)* What are you doing with Mikhail's file?

NOEL: Oh, yeah. *(Opening file)* Does anybody know why he suddenly gets a T V after six years in the West?

HARRY: He likes chess.

JEREMY: They're broadcasting the Fischer-Spassky match from Iceland.

NOEL: Ohhh. ...What were you saying about me?, if I may ask.

JEREMY: That you should take on the bear. You and Sylvia.

NOEL: I was going to suggest that.

JEREMY: You're new. Your cover is intact. It's a good idea.

HARRY: *(Not pleased, hands* NOEL *file)* Well, here. You'll want this.

NOEL: Who's this?

HARRY: *(Snorts)* Ivan.

NOEL: Mikhail's sidekick?

HARRY: Yeah. He's a doozy. The Kremlin gives these guys about nine bucks to live on, so Ivan is always trying to save money. Today he decides he'll save money on gasoline if he coasts down hill. He turns off the engine, the steering wheel locks, he drives off the highway into a brick wall.

NOEL: Was he hurt?

HARRY: They don't get hurt.

JEREMY: We got a directive this morning. H Q wants us to step up our efforts on Mikhail.

NOEL: Has something happened?

JEREMY: Yes. Moscow is focusing a lot of time and money on something or somebody called "Raven."

NOEL: What is it?

JEREMY: It may have something to do with the Israelis.

NOEL: What to do with the Israelis?

HARRY: Well, if we knew that—

JEREMY: That's the point. Nobody knows.

NOEL: We have Mikhail's office bugged.

HARRY: They don't talk about it in the office.

NOEL: Then where did we hear about Raven and the Israelis—it sounds like a band.

HARRY: It's out of Moscow.

JEREMY: H Q wants us to focus on Munich.

NOEL: The Olympics?

JEREMY: The King Tut Exhibit.

HARRY: Mikhail likes art. He hits every major exhibit.

NOEL: Is he going to take his wife... *(Reading)* Varya?

JEREMY: Probably.

NOEL: Then let's plan on me and Sylvia making contact in Munich.

*(*HARRY *chuckles, brief pause.)*

JEREMY: It's very unlikely that you can make contact. I would say it most likely...can't be done.

NOEL: The point *is* to make contact, isn't it?

JEREMY: The point is to *try*. No one expects us to succeed.

NOEL: If I'm not going to make contact, why schlep Sylvia all the way to Munich? Why *drag* her all the way to Munich?

JEREMY: I know what schlep means.

HARRY: ...You Jewish?

NOEL: No, I'm—no. It's an expression.

HARRY: Because we work a lot on Saturdays.

NOEL: I said no.

HARRY: Sundays too, come to think of it.

JEREMY: Alright, boys. You *drag* Sylvia to Munich because we got a *directive*. Take advantage of it; take Sylvia to the Olympics, see the King Tut exhibit.

NOEL: We should plan the operation based on an assumption of success.

HARRY: Now look here, Buddy—

JEREMY: I've watched him for five years. He holds everybody at arm's length.

NOEL: Then drop him. Focus on whatshisname in Dortmund.

JEREMY: Whatshisname in Dortmund reports to Mikhail.

HARRY: As does every other Russian in the west.

JEREMY: Mikhail is the target.

HARRY: Everybody else is cheese.

NOEL: Okay. Okay. *(Thinks out loud)* He likes chess. *(Rhetorical)* What else?

HARRY: Beautiful women.

NOEL: Right, with a lot of hair. *(Rhetorical)* And how does that manifest itself?

HARRY: He talks to them.

NOEL: He talks to them; he walks up to them and initiates conversation. What happens when Sylvia and I just happen to be staying in the same Munich hotel as Mikhail and Varya? When he comes down for breakfast, he'll notice this beautiful woman in animated conversation with her husband. He'll see her *again* at the exhibit. In the afternoon, he'll see her deeply involved in a game of chess in the hotel lobby. By dinner, he'll have to talk to her, believe me, he won't be able to resist.

JEREMY: *(Getting caught up) You* can't initiate conversation; he has to speak first.

NOEL: I know that.

JEREMY: Write up the abstract. We'll send it to H Q so they have it on file. Is Sylvia set with alias documentation?

HARRY: Of course.

NOEL: We should do it in true name.

JEREMY: It's not worth the risk.

NOEL: Now, wait a minute, the point is to establish contact, continuing contact. How can I do that if I'm pretending to be some oil executive or a traveling salesman?

HARRY: Why risk your whole career?

NOEL: I'm supposed to become the guy's best friend, have him over for dinner, meet the wife, shoot the breeze, exchange birthday presents, *presents,* for Pete's sake. How are we supposed to become buddy buddies if I can't even give him my true telephone number?

JEREMY: *(He pours himself a glass of wine.)* You're really hooked, aren't you?

NOEL: ...I admit it. I like the rush.

JEREMY: There's nothing like plunking yourself down on the enemy's sofa.

NOEL: In true name.

JEREMY: *(Impressed)* Maybe I need to spend a couple years on the front.

HARRY: *Viet Nam* is not the front.

NOEL: No, but it was mighty instructive.

JEREMY: Not to mention the perks.

NOEL: Hey, I didn't deal the black market—

JEREMY: I was referring to the abundance of young women.

NOEL: ...Oh yeah.

HARRY: This is the real war, Noel. Europe.

NOEL: Hey, I know.

HARRY: *This* is the front.

JEREMY: No, you're right, Harry. Viet Nam is a mistake; there shouldn't be any actual Americans there.

HARRY: No. *Our* Vietnamese should be fighting *their* Vietnamese.

JEREMY: Killing two birds with one stone.

NOEL: I hear Nixon's starting to sweat the demonstrations.

JEREMY: The President is not worried about a few hippies singing on the mall.

NOEL: A million is not a few.

HARRY: No, it didn't matter. I was five blocks away, having dinner at the Flagship, and Main Avenue wasn't even congested.

JEREMY: The voting majority doesn't demonstrate. The President will be re-elected.

HARRY: You and Sylvia get your ballots?

NOEL: We did. *(To* JEREMY*)* That Sylvia—very conscientious. Thanks, by the way, Mary taking her under her wing. That's great.

JEREMY: I didn't have anything to do with it.

NOEL: No, it's great.

JEREMY: Mary figures these things out by herself. It's her niche. Once a company wife finds her niche, she can cope.

NOEL: Sylvia is coping just fine.

JEREMY: *(Pontificates)* The job is brutal on wives. It's the deception, it takes on a life of its own. It starts out to protect her. She won't like knowing I'm trying to recruit a pedophile, so I don't tell her. She won't like knowing somebody is nice to *her* because they're trying to get to *me*, so I don't tell her. She won't like knowing our car is followed all over town, so I don't tell her. In the end, there's a whole lot more I don't tell her than I do tell her. Pretty soon I stop telling her anything at all, for fear of telling her the wrong thing. ...Of course, with Sylvia, it won't be a problem.

NOEL: *(Pause)* So, we can go in true name?

JEREMY: No. I'm going to lunch.

*(*JEREMY *exits.* HARRY *sneers at* NOEL.*)*

HARRY: What a guy. No sacrifice is too great. Even the marriage bed.

NOEL: ...It's a demanding job.

HARRY: Full of stress.

NOEL: So, what do you do, Harry? For stress?

HARRY: Simple things. Sex with my *wife*, a couple drinks, a few sleeping pills.

NOEL: In that order?

HARRY: That's the only order possible.

*(*HARRY *exits.* NOEL *looks at the file.)*

NOEL: Chess...and beautiful women. I don't see how we can fail.

Scene Six

*(*MIKHAIL *and* VARYA *in their apartment. A newspaper. They look at her ring. They speak Russian.)*

MIKHAIL: Ivan for me picked it out. He said ring nicest thing they sell at exhibit. You sure it you like, Varya?

VARYA: I it *love,* Mikhail.

MIKHAIL: Real Nefertiti I saw.

VARYA: In Berlin, no?

MIKHAIL: In West Berlin. Always big crowd. Germans very fascinated by Egyptology.

VARYA: *(Looking at ring)* She so young.

MIKHAIL: All died young.

VARYA: She was Mrs King Tut?

MIKHAIL: No; she was stepmother and mother-in-law.

VARYA: Both?

MIKHAIL: Both.

VARYA: ...Not bury *me* with *your* mother.

MIKHAIL: No, she with him not buried; her statue from another tomb.

VARYA: Then why they sell her at King Tut exhibit?

MIKHAIL: They capitalists, not historians.

VARYA: ...What more they sell?

MIKHAIL: Varyaaaa—

VARYA: I want to *know.* I not corrupted, Mikhail. Tell me what they sell.

MIKHAIL: I not *know* what they sell.

VARYA: Ivan tells you everything in deepest detail, you say that he tells you.

MIKHAIL: What they sell trinkets. It all trinkets.

VARYA: Nothing bad about trinkets.

MIKHAIL: Maybe after more time in west, you start to see problem with trinkets.

VARYA: Will you take me to Munich? To exhibit?

MIKHAIL: It very crowded. Ivan waited and waited. Long lines.

VARYA: I know *lines,* Mischa.

MIKHAIL: We will see.

VARYA: I not have enough to do.

MIKHAIL: You have one whole city to visit; one language to practice. You and Anna practice German.

VARYA: Anna child. She only talks about cosmetics. Her idea of amusement to take me shopping for cosmetics. She wants that I wear false eyelashes.

MIKHAIL: ...How it look?

VARYA: False eyelashes will not make me twenty-five, Mikhail. ...But if you want, I some will get.

MIKHAIL: I joke.

VARYA: I want time with you. You say you have too much work—let me help more. I can do typing.

MIKHAIL: *(Sarcasm)* Kremlin love when wife type secrets.

VARYA: I not tell secrets.

MIKHAIL: You not supposed to know secrets. Where newspaper?

VARYA: Can we on subject stay please?

MIKHAIL: I want to read what written about match.

VARYA: Match you *saw.* You watched them play until draw after three hours and forty-five minutes.

MIKHAIL: I want to know if anybody else thinks American cheats with electronics.

VARYA: You only person in world thinks that.

MIKHAIL: No, it widely held view.

VARYA: You obsessed with match.

MIKHAIL: No. I want also to read about Nixon.

VARYA: Nixon busy firing cabinet.

MIKHAIL: What written about burglary?

VARYA: *(Sarcastic)* "No one employed in White House involved with break-in."

MIKHAIL: You think true?

VARYA: Yes. Now that he fired three people.

(They nod and smile.)

Scene Seven

*(*SYLVIA *in her apartment, wine stain on her blouse. Starts to dial phone. A knock)*

SYLVIA: Oh, gee. Sorry Mom. *(Hangs up)* Coming.

(Enter FRAU RICHTER *with a bottle of wine.)*

FRAU: I am not you disturbing?

SYLVIA: No no, come in come in. I was just um—

FRAU: I brought wine so we ein little chat haben can.

SYLVIA: Oh, um. Swell. Great. *(Gets glasses, pills)*

FRAU: So, are you und dein Herr to die Olympics going?

SYLVIA: There's been some talk of it.

FRAU: It is ganz hard reservations to get.

SYLVIA: I think Noel somebody knows. *(Gives wine, sits.)*

FRAU: Oh. Well. Das ist sehr different; if you somebody *know*.

SYLVIA: I just meant—...I what I meant don't know.

FRAU: There a lot of disappointed people are. People who can't eine ticket to see an Olympic event get. Not even *eine* ticket.

SYLVIA: That too bad is.

FRAU: Deutsche people who are perfectly capable of a ticket buying, are not allowed one to buy, whereas foreign people that aren't even from here someone *know*. Do you think das fair is?

SYLVIA: It doesn't...sound fair.

FRAU: Ja. It isn't. It's been sehr long since the Olympics here were.

SYLVIA: Oh, yeah, Jesse Owens. I mean—Ha!

FRAU: A very great athlete.

SYLVIA: Oh, ja.

FRAU: Part German.

SYLVIA: No.

FRAU: Ja.

SYLVIA: No.

FRAU: Ja. *(Explanation)* I distantly related to Jesse Owens am. Und I German am. So he part German is.

SYLVIA: I don't think it works like that.

FRAU: ...Pardon?

SYLVIA: Sorry, a little English out of me slipped.

FRAU: Germans a remarkable people are.

SYLVIA: Well, two world wars—

FRAU: Es war nothing standing in das country twenty-five years ago. In invention und innovation. We unsurpassed are.

SYLVIA: What about the Japanese—?

FRAU: It won't be long before we surpass even your country.

SYLVIA: Oh, no. No. I don't think so. No.

FRAU: Ja? Then probably you should at a few graphs of gross national product look.

(Enter NOEL *carrying a garment bag.)*

NOEL: Hi, Hon. Oh. Guten tag.

FRAU: Guten Tag, aufwiedersehen. Bye bye. *(Exits)*

NOEL: ...What was that?

SYLVIA: I don't know. I think she wanted to talk economics.

NOEL: Did she show you her graphs?

SYLVIA: Almost. ...Noel?

NOEL: Yes, Hon.

SYLVIA: Are we speaking English?

NOEL: Yeees. Are you alright?

SYLVIA: Fine.

NOEL: *(Concerned, a hug)* Okay. You take care of yourself.

SYLVIA: I do. *(Kisses him)* ...Noel, have you told people I'm Jewish?

NOEL: You're not really Jewish. Not *Jewish* Jewish.

SYLVIA: I think we should tell people.

NOEL: People don't have to know everything about us.

SYLVIA: You didn't have to hear Mary's diamond conspiracy theory.

NOEL: Don't worry, Hon. Your kaffee klatch days are numbered.

SYLVIA: Why?

NOEL: A guy alone—that's old hat. It's you and me in the field.

SYLVIA: ...What field?

NOEL: You'll be great, and it's going to be good for us, too. I don't want you to end up like Mary.

SYLVIA: There's nothing wrong with Mary.

NOEL: I believe Jeremy has abandoned the marriage bed.

SYLVIA: What's *that* mean?

NOEL: They don't have sex anymore.

SYLVIA: Well, you don't have to say it like that. "Abandoned the marriage bed." Makes it sound like some kind of *good* thing. Some noble thing. I don't think it's a good thing. I don't think Mary thinks it's a good thing.

NOEL: Mary has her niche.

SYLVIA: Her *niche*? Her *niche*? What is her *niche*? Is that some kind of *device*, her niche?

NOEL: Hon—

SYLVIA: Because maybe all us wives should get a niche—

NOEL: Hon!

SYLVIA: If our husbands are going to "abandon the marriage bed."

NOEL: ...I'm sorry.

SYLVIA: What are *you* sorry for? Have *you* "abandoned the marriage bed?" Because, if you *have*, don't worry about me, I'll borrow Mary's niche.

NOEL: I need to have some of what you're drinking.

SYLVIA: *(Offers pills)* Then you'll want one of these.

NOEL: ...Are you going to be able to go out tonight?

SYLVIA: *(Shakes pill bottle)* Well, sure, plenty left.

NOEL: Can I see your purse?

SYLVIA: Here. *(Sarcasm)* What is mine is yours.

NOEL: Hon. Please.

SYLVIA: It's been a long day.

NOEL: I've had a long day, too.

SYLVIA: *(Breath)* I'm sorry. *(Breath)* ...I *like* Mary. I like Lila, too. She's Harry's wife.

NOEL: *(Looks in purse)* I know.

SYLVIA: What are you looking for?

NOEL: I put—here it is. I'm testing this equipment.

SYLVIA: You're—? You hid the *little guy* in my purse?

NOEL: Hon, I'm testing equipment.

SYLVIA: In my *purse*? You're testing recording equipment in my *purse*? *My* purse?

NOEL: It's a test.

SYLVIA: You spied on your wife?!

NOEL: I gotta see if it works—

SYLVIA: I don't care if it works. Give me that tape.

NOEL: Why? ...What's *on* it?

SYLVIA: Nothing's *on* it. Give it to me.

NOEL: Here. *(Pause)* Sorry. *(Pause)* Would you do me a favor?

SYLVIA: Ask me some other day!

NOEL: It's important, Hon.

SYLVIA: I bet.

NOEL: ...We save people's lives. We plant a bug, we get information, and we save people's lives.

SYLVIA: *(Exhale)* Show me how.

NOEL: Put the tape in, push rewind, push play. *(Pause)* Okay. I'll go change. You have to get dressed, too, you know.

SYLVIA: I know!

*(*NOEL *exits with garment bag.* SYLVIA *plays tape, speaks over taped voices.)*

SYLVIA: *(Voice on tape)* Where's the bathroom? I've spilled all over myself.

SYLVIA: *(Looks at stain, over the tape)* I don't believe this.

MARY: *(Tape)* That way.

LILA: *(Tape, brief pause)* What do you think?

MARY: *(Tape)* She's a sweet little thing.

LILA: *(Tape)* She's goofy.

SYLVIA: *(Over the tape)* Goofy! I'm goofy?

LILA: *(Tape)* She's got a lot to learn about marriage. And life in the fast lane, and she's just a little naive, wouldn't you say?

SYLVIA: *(Over the tape)* Oh great. I'm goofy and I'm naive.

MARY: *(Tape)* I don't know. Maybe she is a little. ...Lila. Don't you think you've had enough of that?

SYLVIA: *(Over the tape)* I think I've had enough.

LILA: *(Tape)* Oh, you're just like Harry, you give me wine then lecture me for drinking it. Are you going to ration me? That's what Harry does.

MARY: *(Tape)* You have to drive.

(SYLVIA stops tape. Takes tape from machine.)

SYLVIA: *(Sad)* Noel. Your equipment works. It works just fine.

(Enter KING TUT, wearing famous mask and a loin cloth; he is a little confused. SYLVIA is startled.)

SYLVIA: *(She thinks he's NOEL.)* What are you—jeez! make a little noise when you enter a room!

TUT: I made a little noise.

SYLVIA: And don't go springing *outfits* on people.

TUT: It's all I have.

SYLVIA: *(Looks at clothes)* You didn't say it was costumes. ...You look great in that. Where did you get it?

TUT: I've always had it. I'm a little tired of it.

SYLVIA: No, you look cute. The body makeup's perfect. Very sexy.

TUT: *(Embarrassed)* Well, thank you, but I really don't think we should—

SYLVIA: No, we should. Let me touch this mummy.

(They lay down. She kisses him all over.)

TUT: Please—I really need to know—

SYLVIA: Don't worry. Your tape worked just fine.

TUT: I don't want to talk about *tape*. I've had it up to here with tape, thank you.

SYLVIA: *(Relieved)* Oh, good. I hated that tape, really.

TUT: Um...I just wanted to say—I've been waiting a long long time for you.

SYLVIA: You haven't been "waiting a long long time." Last night is pretty recent.

TUT: Sooo long. And suddenly, last night, *you*, saying my name.

SYLVIA: You like me to say your name before you, you know, come.

TUT: I couldn't have come if you hadn't said my name.

SYLVIA: I never knew that, you should have told me.

TUT: I need your help.

SYLVIA: I thought it was all *my* problem.

TUT: Oh no. It's my problem.

SYLVIA: I've never seen you so—*(Hugs him tight)* What is it?! Tell me.

TUT: You know things about me.

SYLVIA: I've tried to learn. I know I fumble around a lot.

TUT: You're the only one who can do it.

SYLVIA: What is it? Just tell me what it is, I'll do it right now.

TUT: What do you *think*? I want you to do the Egyptians.

SYLVIA: *(Worried)* Do...*what* to the Egyptians?

TUT: Your dissertation.

SYLVIA: *(Relieved)* Oh. I thought you wanted me to do some weird sex thing to some Egyptians.

TUT: I can't rest. You gotta open that can of worms.

SYLVIA: *(Confused)* What? Do you mean King Tut?

TUT: *(Bows)* Himself supreme.

SYLVIA: No, I told you I can't do King Tut.

TUT: You're my only hope.

SYLVIA: Oh, Noel.

(She kisses him passionately, knocking off his mask. Enter NOEL *wearing a tuxedo.)*

NOEL: Could you do these stays for me? I'll never get the hang of this. *(Beat, shocked)* What are you doing? —with your tongue—

TUT: *(To* SYLVIA*)* You have to help me.

NOEL: *(To* SYLVIA*)* Help you with what, Hon?

TUT: ...I *really need* to lie down. *(Exits)*

NOEL: *(To* SYLVIA*)* Well, sure. We can "lie down," but tell me, what is it turned you on? Is it the tux, or what?

Scene Eight

(MARY's *apartment.* JEREMY, *in a tuxedo,* MARY *off)*

JEREMY: Did Lila hit the sauce again?

MARY: *(Off)* We all had wine, Jeremy.

JEREMY: In the middle of the day. *(Tisks)* Sylvia drank, too?

MARY: *(Off)* We all had wine, Jeremy.

JEREMY: Have you seen my cufflinks?

MARY: *(Off)* In the pocket.

JEREMY: Oh, here they are. This still fits. What is this tux, about fifteen years old? Still looks good. This was a good investment. Expensive and in good taste. It pays to invest in quality.

(MARY *enters. She wears a sexy, low-cut gown.)*

MARY: We got it on our first tour.

JEREMY: Where did you get—? *(Pause)* Is that new?

MARY: Uh huh.

JEREMY: Are you—are you going to wear it?

MARY: I thought I would.

JEREMY: I've never seen you—um—? ...Are you wearing a bra?

MARY: No. You *can't* wear a bra with a dress like this. Do you like it?

JEREMY: I don't know—I don't know. Um. I don't know.

MARY: Sylvia convinced me. I could never myself. She did my hair, too.

JEREMY: Noel thinks you're taking her under your wing.

MARY: She wouldn't stay under a wing. She convinced me to try on this dress. It reminds me of skinny dipping.

JEREMY: *(Worried)* What skinny dipping?

MARY: Not recently. From when I was a girl. The air on my breasts reminds me. It feels so...foreign. I mean, you'd think a bathing suit wouldn't make any difference, it's so little. But it does. It makes a big difference. *(Brief pause)* I like the way the air feels on my skin.

JEREMY: ...There may be dancing tonight—um.

MARY: *(Brief pause)* By "um," do you mean somebody might ask me to dance? Somebody not you?

JEREMY: Well.

MARY: *(Brief pause)* Does "well" mean that I might end up dancing with somebody who isn't you, and my naked breasts will be mere inches away from his suit jacket?

JEREMY: Well...

MARY: I think it will be alright for me to dance with someone who isn't you. But if you're worried about it, we should try it. A sort of dry run.

*(*MARY *embraces him as if to dance. Brief pause.* JEREMY *remembers.)*

JEREMY: Eisenhower.

MARY: ...Eisenhower?

JEREMY: Yes. The second inauguration.

MARY: *(Understands)* My dress.

JEREMY: It was pink. And all shiny.

MARY: Satin.

JEREMY: Yes. And cut out in the back.

MARY: Yes. You tickled me when we danced.

JEREMY: That idiot from support kept trying to cut in.

MARY: You wouldn't let him.

JEREMY: I didn't let anybody.

MARY: Well, somebody might cut in tonight. *(Looks between them)* Does this look like a suitable distance between somebody-not-you and me dancing at a German-American Friendship Society party? Six inches from breast to suit jacket.

JEREMY: Yes. About six.

MARY: Six is the standard. Sometimes a little more, sometimes a little less. I've never had anyone get fresh with me.

JEREMY: You never wore that dress.

MARY: You don't think someone will try to touch my breasts?

JEREMY: You never know.

MARY: But how could he? I'm holding his left hand and his right hand is behind my back.

JEREMY: I don't know.

MARY: He might pull me closer. *(Does)* He might be short. If he were short, he wouldn't have to move his hand to touch my breasts. He might be able to touch them with his...lips.

(Brief pause, then JEREMY *breaks away)*

JEREMY: You should get dressed. We have to go.

*(*JEREMY *exits.* MARY *is alone with her humiliation for a moment.)*

Scene Nine

(The Russian office. MIKHAIL, IVAN *with a cast on his arm. They speak Russian.)*

MIKHAIL: Her ring Varya like.

IVAN: That goooood. Her ring Anna like too.

MIKHAIL: Ivan? You got Anna ring, too?

IVAN: Yes.

MIKHAIL: Not same one, though.

IVAN: Yes. I not want that I show favorites.

MIKHAIL: They have same ring? Varya will see her ring on finger of Anna?

IVAN: It will make bond between them.

MIKHAIL: It will make them both leave ring at home. *(Sigh)* I have recommended you for commendation.

IVAN: For courage?

MIKHAIL: No, for efforts to cut expenses of office. And after week or so, then I will file accident report.

IVAN: Ah. ...That not honest.

MIKHAIL: It honest *enough*. It *timing*. Believe me, Ivan, this in your best interest.

IVAN: It very stupid. Next time I not take out key.

MIKHAIL: There *not* one next time. You not remove keys anymore, Ivan. You not per*fect* this, it not worth it. ...What say message machine tonight?

IVAN: Nothing.

MIKHAIL: Nothing?

IVAN: ...More security at embassy.

MIKHAIL: Whose Embassy?

IVAN: I not know.

MIKHAIL: What you mean, not know?

IVAN: Message cut off.

MIKHAIL: Why message cut off?

IVAN: To save on electric bill, I put machine on timer.

MIKHAIL: Nyet—*(He doesn't know where to start.)* Oh, Ivan. Who trained you? Never mind. Don't. No. You not put machine on *timer*, we miss important message!

IVAN: That one very good point.

MIKHAIL: *(Exasperated)* I think that maybe I will take day or two, take Varya, fly to Munich, see exhibit. I think that good idea.

IVAN: Oh. Certainly. One very good idea.

(As they exit, the amplified sound of a recording tape rewinding.)

Scene Ten

(German-American Friendship Society dance. The American wives. MARY *wears a different dress.)*

MARY: Don't they look magnificent?

LILA: From the back it's impossible to tell them apart.

SYLVIA: *(Hands* MARY *glass while she goes into purse for pill)* Hold this a second.

LILA: What are those pills you're always taking?

SYLVIA: So I'm invisible. I've had a lot of them today.

MARY: What are you drinking, Lila?

LILA: It's Coke. Okay? Coca-Cola. Very American, very wholesome. *(About the men)* I am jealous of tuxedos. There ought to be an official female festive outfit. I hate this frenzy every time we go someplace about what I wore last time, and who's going to be there and have they already seen my finery? A uniform. A tuxe*da*.

MARY: Jeremy couldn't find me if I was dressed like everybody else.

SYLVIA: Oh! What did he say about your...dress?

MARY: He liked it...very very much.

LILA: Are you blushing?

MARY: I suppose I must be.

LILA: You are. What happened?

MARY: He liked it too much to let me wear it in front of other men. And of course, he reminded me of propriety. *(To* SYLVIA*)* We have to uphold our propriety and we can't do it in low-cut dresses.

SYLVIA: Oh. Is my dress too low cut?

MARY: I'm sure it was fine before you were married, but now you have to be concerned with propriety.

LILA: God, Mary, *can* the propriety already. Let's go to the bar.

(They exit as their husbands approach.)

LILA: Right back.

HARRY: *(To Lila)* Yeah okay. *(Continuing his tirade)* No, see they *give* the formula to the hospital. For free. Then the hospital gives the new mother two weeks' supply. Two weeks is enough time for the mother's milk to dry up, so she ends up having to *buy* the formula to feed the baby.

JEREMY: A modest investment that pays off long term.

HARRY: Yeah, but they could test their marketing ploys in countries where people aren't starving.

JEREMY: If you treat a developing nation like an infant, it will never mature.

HARRY: Malnourished people don't mature. They die.

JEREMY: I'm talking about nations, not people. What happened to our wives?

HARRY: Bathroom. Or drinks.

JEREMY: *(Holds stomach)* What was that meat item?

HARRY: Blutwurst or bratwurst. Liverwurst.

NOEL: Don't they grow vegetables in this country?

HARRY: Sure, for export. Have a Tums, Jeremy. *(Hands him one)*

JEREMY: With scotch?

HARRY: Why not?

NOEL: *(To* JEREMY*)* Was there anything today about me and Sylvia going to Munich?

JEREMY: It's a go. Don't know when yet. Stay loose. *(Re* NOEL*'s tux)* So you found the um—

NOEL: Oh, yeah, right where you said. It fits okay, considering I didn't try it on.

HARRY: You should *buy* one. Two three times a year you gotta drag it out. Rentals add up. They last forever. I've had it let out twice.

JEREMY: I got this in '58. Right before Suez. It still fits.

NOEL: But you've had it let out.

JEREMY: No.

NOEL: It looks like it's been let out.

JEREMY: Where?

NOEL: Right here, along the side.

JEREMY: Oh. So it does.

NOEL: But it looks good.

(They all take a long drink.)

NOEL: Did you see the lottery page today?

JEREMY: I hope you're not a gambler, Noel.

NOEL: No no. They've got a Nixon line.

HARRY: Oh yeah, I saw that.

NOEL: Odds on whether he gets thrown out of office.

(The wives arrive.)

HARRY: He isn't going to get thrown out of anything. He wasn't involved.

MARY: Who, Harry?

HARRY: The President.

LILA: Are you talking about the Watergate again?

HARRY: I am. Some people think it's important, Lila.

NOEL: How can you think he's not involved?

HARRY: Look at the polls, man, the polls! Why would he risk it?

NOEL: He's firing everybody in sight.

LILA: Three people; that's not everybody.

HARRY: So you have been following it.

LILA: It's all you talk about.

HARRY: What a wife. *(Gives her a hug)*

(Music plays)

MARY: Oh, listen.

NOEL: Would you like to dance, Mary?

LILA: You're driving everybody away, Harry.

MARY: I'd love to dance, Noel. And Harry, I think your theories are fascinating.

(NOEL and MARY exit.)

LILA: *(To Harry)* I'll dance with you if you promise not to inundate me with theories.

HARRY: Let's do it.

(They exit.)

JEREMY: Mary says you're fitting right in.

SYLVIA: She's been a big help.

JEREMY: And Noel certainly is.

SYLVIA: He'd be pleased to hear that.

JEREMY: I hope you're not finding things too dull, over on the wife side.

SYLVIA: ...No. Not, too.

JEREMY: You'll see action soon enough.

SYLVIA: ...Great.

JEREMY: And in the meantime, just being a wife is helpful. The enemy is very suspicious of a man alone.

SYLVIA: Well. I want to do everything I can to help.

JEREMY: Really? *(Cozy)* The most helpful thing you can do for Noel is keep him on keel.

*(*KING TUT *appears and advances.* SYLVIA *sees.)*

SYLVIA: Oh. Oh, dear, oh no. Is this a costume party?

JEREMY: No, Dear. Costumes are next week.

SYLVIA: So, there's nobody coming over here dressed like King Tut?

JEREMY: *(Laughs)* No, just the usual penguins. ...Noel confides in you, I'm sure.

SYLVIA: We're married.

JEREMY: Yes, it's only natural for a husband to tell his wife secrets.

TUT: It depends on the marriage.

JEREMY: Well, yes, Sylvia, that's certainly true.

TUT: Secrets, confiding—they aren't automatic.

JEREMY: *Does* Noel confide in you?

SYLVIA: *(Fast, so* TUT *can't reply)* Yes! Yes, he does.

JEREMY: I thought so; that's good. You see, there are one or two asterisks in Noel's file.

TUT: Is that bad?

JEREMY: Oh, nothing damaging, nothing that isn't good in its own *way*. He has a lone-wolf mentality that was fine for Viet Nam, but won't wash in Europe. We don't want the boy going off half cocked, now do we?

TUT: We don't?

JEREMY: No, we don't. You should let me know if you suspect any... rogue projects? It'll be just between us, of course.

SYLVIA: *(Fast)* I can't....

JEREMY: Can't what?

SYLVIA: I can't just put the little guy in his pocket!

JEREMY: ...Pardon?

SYLVIA: I'm feeling—must be the wine—could you—?

JEREMY: *(Concerned)* Water? Do you need some water?

TUT: Water! I'd *love* some water.

JEREMY: I'll be right—will you be alright?

(She nods. He exits.)

TUT: *(Outraged)* That man expects you to spy on your husband. He must have a *terrific* marriage.

SYLVIA: You are just some figment! Some figment.

TUT: Are you done?

SYLVIA: Some talking mirage.

TUT: Because if you're done, I'd like to get down to business.

SYLVIA: No! I can't. I only kissed you because I thought you were my husband.

TUT: *(Sarcasm)* Oh yes, your husband and I look exactly alike.

SYLVIA: Away away.

TUT: Identical in every way.

SYLVIA: Noel's never going to understand this.

TUT: Why not? I would.

SYLVIA: Oh sure, some dead guy shows up, starts wooing your wife.

TUT: Dead guys are *nothing;* I had it really tough.

SYLVIA: You had it made, your majesty.

TUT: Ha! You try marrying your older sister when you're eleven years old.

SYLVIA: Well, that's ridiculous.

TUT: I'll say. *(Rhetorical)* What are you supposed to do on your wedding night, play chess?

SYLVIA: What did you do?

TUT: Chess. It was chess until I was twelve.

SYLVIA: What did you do at twelve?

TUT: Whatever she told me.

SYLVIA: She told you?

TUT: Of course, I'd never even *seen* one of those before. Before she told me, it was a lot of fumbling.

SYLVIA: We don't fumble.

TUT: *(Sarcasm)* No, your husband gets you there every single time.

SYLVIA: *(Gasp)* How did you—you—get out of here, go away, right now.

TUT: Can't. I need to know if it was my wife who thwacked me. All of a sudden the lights went out. I'm not going any place until you tell me who murdered me.

SYLVIA: How am I supposed to know that?

TUT: Find out. Dissertate.

*(*JEREMY *with water and* NOEL *enter.)*

NOEL: Hon, are you alright?

SYLVIA: *(Still mad at* TUT*)* Just dandy.

JEREMY: Sorry it took so long. The Germans have never heard of plain water.

TUT: Can I have a sip of that?

(A tug of water between SYLVIA *and* TUT*)*

SYLVIA: Why? Are you all *dried up*?

JEREMY: You're spilling all over your—

SYLVIA: Been hanging out in the desert too long.

JEREMY: Careful—

SYLVIA: Are you simply *parched*?

NOEL: Hon!

SYLVIA: Skin turning into *parch*ment?

NOEL: Jeremy, I just— Can you—? Jeremy. Let me handle this.

JEREMY: My stars.

*(*JEREMY *exits.)*

NOEL: Hon. Hon. What?! What? is the matter with you?

*(*SYLVIA *looks from* NOEL *to* TUT. *Pause)*

SYLVIA: *(Wee voice)* Nothing.

NOEL: *(Great precision)* I'm going to go get our coats. Don't. Don't do anything.

*(*NOEL *exits.* SYLVIA *looks at* TUT *who folds his arms across his chest and smiles at her. Lights fade out.)*

END OF ACT ONE

(Intermission; coffee, snacks; bathroom)

ACT TWO

Scene One

(Next week. The apartment. SYLVIA *with reference book, dressed as Cleopatra, takes a pill, sips wine, talking to* NOEL, *off.)*

SYLVIA: King Tut was murdered by *somebody;* you don't get a crushed skull from walking into a door. After he died, his advisor, this guy named *Ay,* married his widow and helped her with all the burial arrangements.

*(*NOEL *enters wearing King Tut outfit.)*

SYLVIA: *(Continues)* No wonder King Tut put a curse on everybody.

NOEL: There's no curse.

SYLVIA: There certainly is—*(Startled)* What are you—?! Oh!

NOEL: Pretty good, huh?

SYLVIA: Very...authentic.

NOEL: There's no curse. It's a virus or something. You start writing about *The Curse of The Pharaohs* in a dissertation, your committee's going to throw it out the window.

SYLVIA: *(Reading)* Then why did all those tomb raiders die?

NOEL: They weren't tomb raiders; they were archaeologists.

SYLVIA: *(Reading)* Right before he died, King Tut and Ay had a big fight.

NOEL: ...You had a fight with King Tut?

SYLVIA: How did you know?

NOEL: You just said so.

SYLVIA: Oh, no, not me. King Tut and Ay, *Ay*. I told you. His advisor was named *Ay*. *(Spelling)* A. Y. Ay.

NOEL: Uh huh. Did anybody call?

SYLVIA: You would have heard it ring.

NOEL: I was in the shower.

SYLVIA: *(Fed up)* Nobody called while you were in the shower, nobody called while you were on your way home from work, nobody called when you went out to make your phone call. *(Pause)* What is this *call* you're waiting for, Noel?

NOEL: Nothing. *(Pause, explains)* Half the embassies have increased security.

SYLVIA: Yes?

NOEL: Which means they think something is going to happen.

SYLVIA: ...To who?

NOEL: Who knows? Us. The Israelis. The Lebanese.

SYLVIA: Let's call them up.

(She picks up phone.)

NOEL: Let's call who up?

SYLVIA: The half that haven't increased security. Let's warn them.

NOEL: We're not calling anybody. Hon, put down the phone.

SYLVIA: No, I'm gonna call the Israelis and Lebanese.

NOEL: Hon. You got to treat people like adults. Equals. Respect their ability to know what's what. I know what I'm talking about. Really. ...Hon, you don't have to tell an Israeli to watch his back, it's automatic.

SYLVIA: What about the Lebanese?

NOEL: The Lebanese we don't care. *(She puts down phone. A hug)*

NOEL: You look nice.

SYLVIA: I feel stupid. Why are they having this King Tut thing anyway? The exhibit's in Munich.

NOEL: Because the Germans love to dress up like Egyptians.

SYLVIA: Do you have anything on underneath that?

NOEL: No, it's authentic.

SYLVIA: *(Touches his behind)* There may be dancing.

NOEL: Yeah, so?

SYLVIA: You're indecent for dancing.

NOEL: I'll only dance with you. *(A kiss)* Not too scared of King Tut *now,* are you?

SYLVIA: Ha! *(Changes the subject)* Your penis is poking.

NOEL: That's a normal hang.

SYLVIA: It looks like poking.

NOEL: I'll put on underpants.

*(*NOEL *exits. a knock)*

SYLVIA: I'll get it.

(Enter LILA, *also dressed as Cleopatra.)*

LILA: Hi. You look smashing.

SYLVIA: ...I look the same as you.

LILA: I, too, look smashing. What are we drinking?

SYLVIA: ...Oh, it's nothing. The landlady left it.

LILA: Give me a sip. *(Sips)* Pretty bad. Is there anything else?

SYLVIA: Nope.

LILA: Then I'll have some of this.

*(*SYLVIA *reluctantly gives* LILA *wine.)*

LILA: Where's himself?

SYLVIA: Putting on underpants.

LILA: It won't be authentic.

SYLVIA: He was poking. Is Harry wearing underpants?

LILA: Harry is wearing a tuxedo. So is Jeremy, I hear. A tux and the headdress. I long to see it, all the women dressed like Cleopatra, all the men in tuxedos. Perfect.

(A knock)

LILA: I'll get it.

(Enter FRAU RICHTER, *dressed as Cleopatra. She looks remarkably like King Tut.)*

FRAU: Guten abend.

SYLVIA: *(Big shock)* Oh. Oh, no. Oh. No. I need—*(To* LILA*)* Do you see that? That?

LILA: *(To* SYLVIA*)* Are you alright?

FRAU: Abend. I wanted *your* costumes to see. Ich bin die landlady.

LILA: Are you also to the Deutsche-American Friendship Society dance going?

FRAU: Nein. I'm to a King Tut party going. I distantly related to King Tut am.

LILA: Really?

FRAU: Ja, you can das resemblance in my face see.

LILA: ...Tut just never did to me German look.

FRAU: You can't always by looking tell.

LILA: Well, you...smashing look.

FRAU: Ja. You also, but you authentic aren't.

LILA: Why not?

FRAU: Egyptians didn't tops wear-en. You should naked breasts haben.

LILA: *You* don't naked breasts haben.

FRAU: Das top is only for in das taxi wearing. When I there get, I will das top off taken.

LILA: Well, maybe we will our tops off taken, too.

FRAU: That would an improvement make, but you still won't authentic be.

LILA: Why not?

FRAU: Because you *white* are. Ha! Abend. *(Exits)*

LILA: Abend. ...Charming. It would serve Harry right if I didn't wear a top. I have to be authentic and *he's* wearing a tux? What a stuffed shirt. ...Are you okay?

SYLVIA: Fine fine. *(Sips wine, takes pills)*

LILA: Harry told me about you, you slippery little dog. Assistant to the head of something or other.

SYLVIA: If there is some Sylvia who was the assistant to the head of something, I'm sure it's a Sylvia with an "I".

LILA: ...Would you repeat that please?

SYLVIA: No.

LILA: ...Let me see your palm. *(Looks)* Oh, yeah, this is nothing like mine. See this fatty part? That translates into you keep your mouth shut. See mine? All skinny. That means I blab.

SYLVIA: I *do* keep my mouth shut.

LILA: *(Looks)* Look, two marriages.

SYLVIA: No. Where?

LILA: Oh, maybe not. One marriage, but with a definite period of estrangement.

SYLVIA: Does it say I'm goofy?

LILA: ...I don't see goofy.

SYLVIA: You thought I was goofy.

LILA: No, I didn't.

SYLVIA: I thought you thought I was goofy.

LILA: Well, maybe I *did* think it, but I don't think it now, and that's what counts, right? *(Holds out glass)*

SYLVIA: Oh. All gone.

LILA: It isn't all gone, I can see it. ...Have you been talking to Harry?

SYLVIA: I haven't.

LILA: Or reading my file?

SYLVIA: No!

LILA: May I have some more of your too sweet, not very good, leftover wine, please?

SYLVIA: Of course, whatever you like.

LILA: Thank you. I mean, *you* should talk, right?

SYLVIA: Whaddayoumean?

LILA: Here a pill, there a pill, everywhere a pill pill.

SYLVIA: Those pills are *medicine.*

(NOEL enters.)

LILA: Hi, you.

NOEL: I thought we were meeting *there.*

LILA: Harry wants you to call the office. From outside.

NOEL: I better change—

(NOEL exits to bedroom.)

LILA: You certainly better.

SYLVIA: What's happening?

LILA: I'm sure we'll find out later.

SYLVIA: Are we going to miss the party?

LILA: That would be my guess.

SYLVIA: *(Relieved)* Oh, good. *(Gets wine)*

LILA: I know. I hate these quaint local customs.

SYLVIA: Then why do you go?

LILA: What? Stay at home and watch as my husband slips away?

(NOEL enters with a trench coat over his outfit, and exits.)

NOEL: Right back.

LILA: He's cute.

SYLVIA: Um.

LILA: The boys say he acquitted himself nicely in Nam.

SYLVIA: He doesn't talk about it.

LILA: Some sleight-of-hand around a glass of poisoned wine. A very tricky operation.

SYLVIA: We're still not winning.

LILA: It depends on who you talk to. Harry did a tour in Nam. What a circus. Normal, rational guys lost their whole minds.

SYLVIA: ...Noel did *two* tours.

LILA: You must have seen the reports. The drugs, the teenage girls.

SYLVIA: *(Shocked)* How teenage? I mean, nineteen or thirteen?

LILA: If a guy's forty, what difference does it make?

SYLVIA: ...Harry had a teenage girl?

LILA: They all did, I'm telling you, they went nuts—they thought young girls were an inalienable right for action above and beyond the call of duty. Harry, *Harry* was convinced he had to do something spectacular over there if he wanted to get ahead. He was possessed.

SYLVIA: Noel doesn't care about that.

LILA: That's not what I hear. Couple of sweet young things like yourselves. Be everybody's darlings in a few years. *For* a few years. Sometimes I wish he'd bagged it, gone to medical school.

SYLVIA: I can't imagine Harry as a doctor.

LILA: No, he would have been a terrific doctor.

SYLVIA: And what would you have been?

LILA: I would have been the spy. I liked my job.

SYLVIA: Maybe you should go back when your baby grows up.

LILA: I can't go back. You know that.

SYLVIA: I don't. I swear I don't.

LILA: I got canned. I didn't quit to have a baby, I had a baby because I got canned. They wanted me to spy on Harry.

SYLVIA: Oh, I know, me too, on Noel! But you didn't!

LILA: Of course I didn't. I pretended to. They found out. Those guys really can't take a joke.

SYLVIA: Harry should have quit. Gone to medical school. You should have *made* him, you should have.

LILA: What? Screamed "me or the company"?

SYLVIA: Yes, me or the company.

LILA: Too risky.

(NOEL reenters.)

NOEL: *(To LILA)* Harry said he'll meet you there.

LILA: *(Getting up)* Okeydokey. You two coming?

NOEL: No.

LILA: Okeydokey. Ta. *(Exits)*

NOEL: It's a go. Pack for a couple of days.

SYLVIA: *(Worried)* Is it the Israelis?

NOEL: The who? No! The Israelis are fine. Pack like for a weekend.

SYLVIA: I'm going, too?

NOEL: Yeah. Take sexy stuff. Low cut.

SYLVIA: Low cut—What about my propriety?

NOEL: Hon—take low cut.

SYLVIA: Where are we going?

NOEL: I'll tell you in the car. Oh, and do your hair big.

Scene Two

(German-American Friendship Society dance. HARRY in tuxedo, LILA as Cleopatra; a tango.)

HARRY: Who do you pretend you *are*?

LILA: I pretend I'm you.

HARRY: Then who do you pretend I am?

LILA: I pretend you're you, too.

HARRY: I can't picture it. I don't wanna picture it.

LILA: No, you should picture it. It's very sexy. What do *you* pretend?

HARRY: I don't, I told you I don't.

LILA: You think it's *me* doing that stuff?!

HARRY: *(Smile)* It is you.

LILA: Yes, but you're not supposed to pretend that.

HARRY: I pretend all day long. I don't have the energy to pretend at night. Besides, the real thing is okay.

LILA: Thank you, Kind Sir. ...Where are the newlyweds off to?

HARRY: South. Shhh. Very secret.

LILA: Big time assignment, huh?

HARRY: Only if they pull it off.

LILA: How come you didn't get it?

HARRY: *(Lying)* I didn't want it.

LILA: ...Oh.

HARRY: Really.

LILA: No, I believe you. I wonder why, is all.

HARRY: Like I said, no energy.

LILA: Is it me? Is it because of me?

HARRY: *(Lying)* No.

LILA: Harry, you're good at your job.

HARRY: I need a vacation.

LILA: Let's go to Africa.

HARRY: *(Pause)* I was thinking more like America.

LILA: ...Go home?

HARRY: Yeah. Two, four years.

LILA: *(Happy, stops dancing)* Oh, Harry, can we really go home?

HARRY: Yeah. Let things shake out here for a couple years. We come back, and *I'm* the new guy in town.

LILA: Do we have to come back?

HARRY: Yeah. It'll be a whole new ball game.

(Enter MARY, *dressed as Cleopatra. She is drunk.)*

MARY: Can I dance with you?

HARRY: Me?

MARY: Both of you.

HARRY: Sort of clumsy.

MARY: Then just you.

*(*MARY *dances with* LILA.*)*

HARRY: Mary, do you want me to get you something? Water?

MARY: I want to dance.

HARRY: I'll go get Jeremy.

MARY: No. Don't get Jeremy. Get champagne.

HARRY: I'll get champagne. You okay?

LILA: We're fine.

*(*HARRY *exits.* MARY *and* LILA *slow dance.)*

MARY: Do you think Harry would take a bath with me?

LILA: We can ask him.

MARY: Would you take a bath with me?

LILA: Sure.

MARY: Don't humor me. ...I don't know what to do, I don't know what to do.

LILA: Escape.

MARY: They'd find me.

LILA: Not if you change your name.

MARY: An alias! ...No. They'd still find me.

LILA: What if you didn't leave?

MARY: Then what's the point?

LILA: If you don't leave, nobody's looking. Stay home as Mary, send your alias out for some fun.

MARY: Mary Anne.

LILA: Sure, Mary Anne-the-swinger.

MARY: And nobody is looking for *Mary* because she's still there.

LILA: Right where we left her, at home suffering her miserable life, which *Mary Anne* makes up for later.

MARY: She does?

LILA: She can.

MARY: What if *Mary Anne* gets caught?

LILA: Then she just...changes her name.

Scene Three

(A hotel lobby. NOEL *and* SYLVIA, *big hair, low cut dress. A chess set)*

SYLVIA: *(Worried)* Who do we pretend we *are*?

NOEL: Hon, the knight, move the knight.

SYLVIA: Which one is the knight?

NOEL: The one that looks like a horse.

SYLVIA: Then why don't you call it the horse? *(Moves it)*

NOEL: No. Hon, no. You can move it here, here, or here. You can't move it there.

SYLVIA: What are we supposed to say if they talk to us? What if they ask us something? Who are we?

NOEL: If they ask, I'll answer. You're just the wife here.

SYLVIA: Noel—?

NOEL: Ned. Ned. Suzie and Ned. Oh my God. Oh no.

SYLVIA: What? Are you alright?

NOEL: Don't look up. Just focus on the board. Hon, just be cool, just be—

*(*NOEL *exits quickly.)*

SYLVIA: Wait—

*(*MIKHAIL *walks by, glancing at the chess game.)*

MIKHAIL: Guten Tag.

SYLVIA: Guten Tag.

MIKHAIL: Your queen in sehr bad trouble is.

*(*MIKHAIL *exits in the same direction as* NOEL.*)*

SYLVIA: Oy veh.

Scene Four

(A hotel room. NOEL, SYLVIA, MIKHAIL, VARYA. *Wine and vodka. Note: they speak bad German very easily.)*

NOEL: Nein, I just a geologist am. I like with das rocks working. Mein hands dirty getting. The oil company is always trying me to ein desk job promote.

MIKHAIL: Ja. I exactly what you mean know. I also ein desk job hate.

NOEL: We a lot in common have.

MIKHAIL: I das think too. We both desk hate—

NOEL: We both chess like—

MIKHAIL: We both wives to exhibit brought.

VARYA: I question about oil have.

NOEL: What?

VARYA: If so much oil out of ground taken is, why does ground collapse not?

NOEL: Well. You see, das earth round is. It has to do with das physics of roundness. Ja.

VARYA: Ah.

MIKHAIL: *(Brief pause)* Suzie. How did you King Tut exhibit like?

SYLVIA: Once I in was, I it liked. But I almost didn't in *go.*

NOEL: Hon—

SYLVIA: Ned here, had to me a little shove give, ha. But I it loved once I inside was. Das poor little King, but he proved you *can* it with you take.

MIKHAIL: He proved you can your relatives from getting it prevent.

VARYA: It very materialistic.

SYLVIA: Ja, like all the time shopping.

VARYA: Do you das do?

SYLVIA: Not me.

NOEL: We'd rather mountains climb.

MIKHAIL: Very Ernest Hemingway.

SYLVIA: Did you Ernest Hemingway know?

MIKHAIL: Not personally. No.

SYLVIA: I thought since you guys—Cuba? I don't know—

NOEL: *(Interrupts)* I the exhibit loved.

MIKHAIL: Not me.

SYLVIA: No?

NOEL: Not even the bird?

SYLVIA: What bird?

NOEL: The carved ebony bird. What's it called?

MIKHAIL: I not know.

NOEL: Oh, you know, the big bird, black, bigger than a crow. *(Squawks)*

VARYA: ...Raven?

NOEL: Ja, that's it. Beautiful.

VARYA: I not think Raven so beautiful.

MIKHAIL: *(Brief pause)* I not think so also. Art should emotions affect.

SYLVIA: Like das Impressionists.

MIKHAIL: Well, Impressionists somewhat soft are.

SYLVIA: Not Monet.

MIKHAIL: Jawol, all of them. Except pointillist, Seurat.

SYLVIA: It's not too...decadent, is it?

MIKHAIL: Creating one form from many dots very...Soviet. *(Laughs)* My other tastes harder to justify to colleagues. With them, I of chess speak.

SYLVIA: I love chess. I just started—

NOEL: Suzie's learning.

MIKHAIL: *(To* SYLVIA*)* We play must.

SYLVIA: Oh, no. Play with Noel—? Um, nooooo play with Ned. I mean, do you modern art in das Soviet Union have?

MIKHAIL: Ja, und I more examples in west see. ...I another toast make.

SYLVIA: Oh, good, another toast.

(Enter KING TUT.*)*

SYLVIA: *(About* TUT*)* Oy veh—

NOEL: Hon—?

SYLVIA: *(Covering)* Oh, hooray! Hooray. A toast. *(She gets her purse.)* I need...oh, where are they?

(When her purse faces toward MIKHAIL *and* VARYA*; they cover their faces as if they don't want their photo taken, she notices them.)*

SYLVIA: Oh. I was...a pill getting; it's not a—just a purse. *(Puts it down)* I'll now...sit. Well, isn't this amazing. The five of us, uh, *four*, the *four* of us here sitting, wine drinking in a language nobody is sure about. I hardly know what next I going to say am. Why don't you two ein little chess match have? Our own version of a Boris Spassky/Bobby Fischer game.

MIKHAIL: Very allegorical. I can the Russian bear be und you can the American Jew be.

TUT: Jews! We had Jews. Terrific workers. Our Jews built the Pyramids.

VARYA: I didn't know.

SYLVIA: Ja! Das Pyramids. ...I it in some movie saw. Plus das Bible. *(Sings)* Let my people go, ha.

(SYLVIA gives Tut a stern look.)

MIKHAIL: My toast—to the living.

TUT: *(Disappointed)* Aw—

MIKHAIL: *(To SYLVIA) And* to your beautiful hair.

VARYA: Oh, yes, lovely hair.

SYLVIA: Thanks. Ned, here, thinks I should it cut.

TUT: We wore wigs.

MIKHAIL: *(Suspicious)* Wigs, why?

SYLVIA: The *Egyptians* wore wigs.

MIKHAIL: Ned, do not urge that Suzie her beautiful hair cut.

NOEL: Well, it's just, hippies have long hair a bad name given.

MIKHAIL: Ah, yes, your hippies. Interesting.

NOEL: A lot of Americans don't agree.

MIKHAIL: Und you, Ned, how do you about hippies feel?

NOEL: I understand das search. Das need to find meaning beyond "things go better with Coke."

VARYA: Coca-Cola, yes.

MIKHAIL: Varya, please.

VARYA: I like Coca-Cola.

NOEL: *(Heartfelt)* I meant—I their need understand. Das need to more than the sum of your possessions be. Das need to something other than greedy be.

VARYA: Greed very unattractive. Acquisitiveness. Not very Soviet.

NOEL: *(Disdain)* Well, it very American is.

TUT: It's also very Egyptian.

NOEL: *(To SYLVIA)* Hon, please—

VARYA: Me, too, I understand. I not an acquisitive person want to be, but sometimes I fail. Mischa this for me bought. *(Ring)* I admit to being rather fond of it.

NOEL: Is that King Tut in a funny hat?

VARYA: Nefertiti.

TUT: *(Looking at ring)* Oh, I remember that statue; the one that looks like she's wearing a pointy headdress.

VARYA: *(To* SYLVIA*)* *Isn't* she a pointy headdress wearing?

TUT: No. She had a pointy head. An unfortunate result of in-breeding.

MIKHAIL: Ach, ja. They married their daughters.

TUT: And their sisters.

SYLVIA: Nefertiti made King Tut marry her daughter, who was his half sister by his father. Ha.

VARYA: You so much about Egyptians know.

SYLVIA: I'm doing a dissertation on them. Working night and day.

TUT: So there should be some results soon.

NOEL: I didn't know you a topic chose.

SYLVIA: Actually, a topic was on me thrust.

MIKHAIL: Are you about King Tut writing?

SYLVIA: About his murder. As soon as I figure out who it did.

VARYA: Who you suspect?

SYLVIA: It very bad for das wife looks. She all these miscarriages had. She feared His Highness was going her to dump for some teenager.

TUT: It wouldn't have happened. Not in three thousand years.

SYLVIA: Three thousand five hundred.

MIKHAIL: So. I hear that your president in a real jam is.

NOEL: *(Eager)* Where do you that hear?

MIKHAIL: In *Der Spiegel.*

NOEL: I that also read.

MIKHAIL: Ja. It said he should resign.

TUT: He should just retire. Spend some time at home with his wife. Do them both some good.

NOEL: Hon, this about *retirement* isn't. *(To change subject)* I *Der Spiegel* like.

MIKHAIL: Ja, good magazine. Almost as good as *Pravda.*

NOEL: Ja, it has a lot of influence. More than a paper.

MIKHAIL: Oh, ja. A paper has limited influence.

TUT: I love paper. The way it feels.

NOEL: Hon—

TUT: It's a shame to cut down all the papyrus plants, though.

MIKHAIL: *(Brief pause)* Oh. Ha. I get it. Ha. Yes, it shame is to cut down trees for newspaper.

SYLVIA: Ha. Ha ha.

MIKHAIL: I something special have. It's Russian. We shall one real toast have.

(He holds up vodka bottle.)

MIKHAIL: Wine fine, but vodka better. Here, Suzie. Drink it down all at once.

(She does.)

MIKHAIL: Oh. You were for the rest of us to wait. Here. *(He pours another for her, pours others.)*

MIKHAIL: *(Continued)* To us four. May some day our nations come this close to one another.

(They all drink.)

SYLVIA: *(Moved)* That's what I wish. People should get to know each other. And then we wouldn't spying need—I mean, we wouldn't the cold war need. I didn't spying mean.

MIKHAIL: I know what you mean.

NOEL: Hon. You aren't well feeling. We should go.

MIKHAIL: Nonsense, she's fine feeling. Another toast.

NOEL: Another toast. I das bathroom need—

MIKHAIL: It right through—

NOEL: I know. Our room's the same.

*(*NOEL *exits to the bathroom.)*

MIKHAIL: So, Suzie. I'm glad that we met have.

SYLVIA: Ja, me too.

MIKHAIL: We must in touch stay. Give to me your telephone number, please.

SYLVIA: *(Pause as she doesn't know what to do)* ...Who?

MIKHAIL: Your telephone number. What is it?

SYLVIA: Give me *your* telephone number.

MIKHAIL: Certainly. *(Gives her his business card)* My card; five, three, two, one, nine, five. Und yours?

(Pause, all eyes on SYLVIA, *who looks at business card;* TUT *looks at it over her shoulder.)*

TUT: What beautiful paper.

MIKHAIL: Thank you.

TUT: The edges are so square.

MIKHAIL: I think it's standard.

TUT: And it's so cute and little.

MIKHAIL: To fit inside a wallet.

TUT: What's a wallet?

SYLVIA: *(To stop* TUT *from talking) Seven,* O, O, nine, nine, nine.

MIKHAIL: I'm sure we can all together get.

Scene Five

(A hotel room. SYLVIA *and* NOEL *in a very huge bed.* SYLVIA *awakens.)*

SYLVIA: Oh, that was—? Oh—it was a dream.

*(*KING TUT *sits up in the bed.)*

SYLVIA: What are you doing here?

TUT: *(Sheepish smile)* You were wiggling your behind.

SYLVIA: Well, I wasn't wiggling it at you.

TUT: Please.

SYLVIA: I'm doing a dissertation for you. I think that's sufficient.

TUT: You're right. That *is* sufficient and generous. I was overcome. My one chance for human contact before being thrust back to the realm of ephemeral light. Where heat and cold and tender touch are but memory. Adrift in the feelingless cosmos never to have or know—

SYLVIA: *(Fed up)* Oh, stop it. Now just stop it. Come here.

(She gives him a kiss. Another. It heats up. They slip under the sheet. Moans, cries, eventually, she tells him where.)

SYLVIA: Oh. Oh. There! No, *there,* right *there.* Yes! Yes!

(She continues shouting as NOEL *wakes up.)*

NOEL: What? What? Stop shouting, for Pete's sake.

SYLVIA: *(Peeks out from sheet)* What?

NOEL: You're going to wake up the whole hotel.

SYLVIA: What was I doing?

NOEL: You were making elefanten fluken zounden, is what you were doing.

SYLVIA: Well at least I'm not bathing with the neighbors!

NOEL: Hon. Wake up, please. You're having some dream.

SYLVIA: ...Yeah. It was some dream.

NOEL: I feel terrible.

SYLVIA: From the wine. Or the beer.

NOEL: Or the vodka.

(A pause during which they realize they are awake. NOEL *puts his arm around her.)*

NOEL: You okay?

SYLVIA: Sure, *(Lying)* it was just one of those dreams that feels really real. ...How was the chess game?

NOEL: He thrashed me. Fool's mate.

SYLVIA: No.

NOEL: Yeah. I don't care. I out-spied him. It felt great. He never suspected, never.

SYLVIA: *(Whisper)* Is it alright to talk?

NOEL: Yeah, we own the hotel.

SYLVIA: I think he knows.

NOEL: No, he doesn't; he just doesn't. Hon. It was amazing. I beat him to the elevator, that's what did it.

SYLVIA: ...In the lobby?

NOEL: Yeah. It went down exactly like I said it would in my abstract, but the elevator, that was just the right touch. *(He explains.)* I saw him stand up—that's why I ran off.

SYLVIA: Oh, I thought it was bowel trouble. You know how you get when you're nervous.

NOEL: No. No! I was trying to get to the elevator first, so he wouldn't think I was following him. Timing. He had to stop the doors with his hand. If he'd gotten there first, if I'd followed him in, he never would have talked, never would have invited us to his room. ...I got him to say "Raven." I can't believe it.

SYLVIA: He didn't say Raven.

NOEL: He said Raven.

SYLVIA: She said Raven.

NOEL: She said Raven?

SYLVIA: Yeah.

NOEL: Well. As long as somebody said it. I was focused. All day, wound like a clock, if he farted I would have known it. When he talked to that guy at the museum, I saw his cheek twitch I just knew it.

SYLVIA: The guy who looked like an Arab guestworker?

NOEL: Yeah. Mikhail got news. His face fell about four feet.

SYLVIA: I didn't notice. *(Pause)* Noel. You know. What you said about searching—understanding the hippies—I know what you mean. I want my life to be more than the sum of my possessions.

NOEL: What—? Oh, Hon. That was—I didn't mean that. Understand the hippies? They're fanatics. They should be in jail.

SYLVIA: You mean you were lying?

NOEL: Hon! I was in Viet Nam!

SYLVIA: I know. What happened to your teenage girl?

NOEL: My teenage girl?

SYLVIA: Yes! What happens to those teenagers when their Americans go home?

NOEL: It's a war. No teenage girl!

SYLVIA: ...I thought you had a teenage girl.

NOEL: *(Lying)* Of course I didn't. And even if I did, so what? *You're* my wife now. My lawfully wedded wife.

(He holds her hand. They look at her wedding ring.)

SYLVIA: Did you see her ring?

NOEL: I saw it. Twelve marks max.

SYLVIA: She was so proud of her dinky little, twelve-mark ring.

NOEL: You have a one-carat flawless diamond ring.

SYLVIA: She was so proud.

NOEL: You're proud of your ring.

SYLVIA: I don't think so.

NOEL: *(Mad)* Well, this is a real problem if you're not proud of your ring. That's a four-thousand-dollar ring. You should be proud. I mean, so? What's the point, Hon?

SYLVIA: How can you call me "Hon" when you're mad at me? "Hon" is supposed to mean you love me, and you don't sound like you love me now.

NOEL: I love you! You should be proud of your ring.

SYLVIA: You call me "Hon" so you won't call me the wrong name when we're lying to some Russians. It isn't about love at all.

(Brief pause, NOEL *is stunned.)*

SYLVIA: Or so you don't scream out some wrong girl's name in the middle of sex. *(Imitating his cry of passion)* "Hon, oh Hon." You probably scream "Oh Hon" for all your girlfriends. "Hon" probably reminds you of your Vietnamese teenager. *(Without a beat)* I gave him our telephone number.

NOEL: Gave who our telephone number?

SYLVIA: You left the room. I had to.

NOEL: Who—?

SYLVIA: Mikhail. How dare you leave me alone with them?

NOEL: Which telephone number?

SYLVIA: Our one.

NOEL: No. *(Slight twitch)* Not our one.

SYLVIA: Yes. I sensed it was a mistake.

NOEL: No—No, Hon, not our one. We were not in true name!

SYLVIA: What's that mean?

NOEL: We had six months of what true name means! You *sensed* it was a mistake?!

SYLVIA: When—

NOEL: Six months! Hon, how could you?

SYLVIA: I didn't have six months of anything, Noel. I had ten weeks of language training—gutan Tag mein Herr. Wie gehts?

(A long long pause. They stare at each other, both realizing NOEL *has made a mistake in his mind.)*

SYLVIA: *(Realization, gasp)* I'm not the Silvia with an "I".

NOEL: —No, I know.

SYLVIA: No, you forgot. You forgot your own Sylvia.

NOEL: No, I love you.

SYLVIA: *(Sad)* You forgot me.

NOEL: It's not what you think.

SYLVIA: *(Sad)* How could you possibly know what Sylvia with a "Y" thinks?

NOEL: *(Big remorse)* Hon, hon. Please, please listen to me. My brain just tripped or something. This ...thing I do, it's not like anything else. When I'm getting ready to go into enemy territory, these drums start beating in my head, like I'm going into battle.

SYLVIA: It's your heart.

NOEL: Maybe it is, but whatever it is, it makes other things, things that aren't the battle, hard to remember.

SYLVIA: I'm the Sylvia with a "Y."

NOEL: I know who you are. I won't forget any more.

Scene Six

(A park. MIKHAIL *and* VARYA, *speaking Russian.)*

VARYA: I not agree they trick us.

MIKHAIL: Was trick.

VARYA: If trick, why he have wife along?

MIKHAIL: Varya. You along.

VARYA: Mischa, I spy only so people not think *you* spy. His technique very old and tired, to criticize own country. Professional spy would laugh at this.

MIKHAIL: He could know that I would think that.

VARYA: Now you sound like K G B manual, Mikhail. "He'll think that I'll think that he'll think that I'll think." Such thinking gives me vertigo.

MIKHAIL: His anti-materialism treatise was very weak.

VARYA: Yes, and professional would fabricate idea more thoroughly. Only true believer so unprepared to extemporize as Ned.

MIKHAIL: She said "spying." Several times.

VARYA: Yes, and professional never would.

MIKHAIL: He said "raven."

VARYA: ...He not say "raven."

MIKHAIL: I heard "raven."

VARYA: I said raven. What means raven?

MIKHAIL: You not want to know.

VARYA: Mikhail, you spoke to him *first*. You came into elevator *after* he came. It very hard to follow from in front; it one of first things they teach you.

MIKHAIL: You not need to speak sarcastic.

VARYA: You have number of telephone. You can call.

MIKHAIL: For somebody not materialistic he bought wife one very big diamond.

VARYA: Maybe she materialistic.

(Enter IVAN.*)*

VARYA: Hello, Ivan.

IVAN: Hello. I sure I wasn't followed.

MIKHAIL: Not important, Ivan.

IVAN: Not important?

MIKHAIL: No. We work in same office; we arrive in country on same day; it perfectly regular you meet with me.

IVAN: That one very good point.

MIKHAIL: Varya, take walk.

VARYA: ...Where?

MIKHAIL: *(Harsh)* Put money in meter.

VARYA: *(Defiant)* How many minutes?

MIKHAIL: Five minutes only.

*(*VARYA *exits, reluctantly.)*

IVAN: You enjoy exhibit?

MIKHAIL: Somewhat. I want that you send cable. It go Top Secret, First Priority, to Andropov.

IVAN: *(Stands at attention)* Andropov!

MIKHAIL: Ivan, sit down.

IVAN: I never have sent cable to head of K G B. What cable about? Goofy Americans you meet in Munich?

MIKHAIL: No, it not about them. Ivan, sit. Say in cable I made contact with Raven.

IVAN: Who he?

MIKHAIL: He our contact in Black September.

IVAN: Ah, yes, Black September.

MIKHAIL: We spoke at King Tut exhibit.

IVAN: Such bold meeting.

MIKHAIL: No. Public meeting safe if look casual. He said attempt will occur to assassinate members of Israeli Olympic team.

IVAN: *(Speechless for a moment)* You think true?

MIKHAIL: Maybe. That explain security around embassies.

IVAN: Will we tell Israelis?

MIKHAIL: I not know. If not true, if trick, we endanger life of Raven.

IVAN: I very nervous.

(Reenter VARYA.*)*

VARYA: Meter have time left.

MIKHAIL: Ivan, go office. I meet you and help with cable.

IVAN: Oh thank you, thank you.

*(*IVAN *bows and exits. A pause.* MIKHAIL *puts head in hands.)*

MIKHAIL: Oy veh—

VARYA: ...What?

MIKHAIL: Nothing. It nothing.

VARYA: *(Worried)* Tell me.

MIKHAIL: I can't.

VARYA: You know I have good ideas.

MIKHAIL: This I can't tell you.

VARYA: I not like this.

MIKHAIL: Varya, no! Will have to wait.

Scene Seven

(The apartment. SYLVIA *and* TUT *intimate on sofa. A glass of wine)*

SYLVIA: There's nobody to talk to in Germany, and I can't call anybody in America because my phone is probably tapped, I mean why else does Noel go out to pay phones, unless, of course, he's calling some *teenage girl.*

TUT: Can we talk about something besides your marriage?

SYLVIA: What else is there?

TUT: *My* marriage!

SYLVIA: I'm working on it, all right?! Drink some wine.

TUT: *(Snippy)* No thanks. The last time I had wine, I died.

SYLVIA: Yeah, it doesn't agree with me either.

TUT: It was right before the *unknown assailant* smashed my head in.

SYLVIA: Alright, already.

TUT: I keep going over everything they said, every pause that was too long, every intimate glance between people I thought were strangers—

SYLVIA: I get more reference books next week.

TUT: I'd overhear Ay say something peculiar, then when I asked him, he denied it.

SYLVIA: Oh, I've had that.

TUT: Looked me square in the face and denied what I just heard.

SYLVIA: Yeah, Noel looked them square in the face and said he didn't like materialism.

TUT: He was lying.

SYLVIA: Lying, yeah, and there was only one other time I saw him look that sincere.

TUT: When he asked you to marry him.

SYLVIA: Yeah. *(Shocked)* How did you—?

TUT: *(Pointedly)* Maybe he was lying then, too.

SYLVIA: You're making me mad, your highness.

TUT: *(Pointedly)* I never lied to *my* wife. I never used her to get ahead in my *job.*

SYLVIA: What?!

TUT: I was planning *to retire.* Early retirement so we could spend more time together.

SYLVIA: *(Mad)* Nobody gives up being a god just to spend more time with some wife.

TUT: In a second.

SYLVIA: Well. *Noel* would retire for *me.*

TUT: *(Sarcasm)* Oh yeah sure.

SYLVIA: He *would.* He loves me more than this stupid job.

TUT: He won't give up his job. For *anybody.*

SYLVIA: He will.

TUT: He doesn't even know which Sylvia he married.

SYLVIA: He does too. The only thing Noel doesn't know is that he's going to medical school.

TUT: I'm sure he'll be thrilled to find out.

SYLVIA: I'll finish my dissertation. Get a teaching job to support him while he gets his degrees—I gotta go over there—

TUT: Go over where?

SYLVIA: I gotta tell him.

TUT: What about *me*?

SYLVIA: You're out of the picture. I can't support two husbands on a teacher's salary.

Scene Eight

(The office. NOEL, *with a typed report, and* JEREMY.*)*

JEREMY: It was your actual, true telephone number?

NOEL: I got caught up in the moment and tripped over my brain. Before I knew what I was doing I heard myself giving him my true telephone number.

JEREMY: Well. *(Pause)* Well. Hum. I'm sure H Q will have an opinion about this.

NOEL: Are you going to send a cable?

JEREMY: No. A cable is bad timing. We'll stay calm, send the report tomorrow or the next day in the pouch. If we send a cable, they'll think we're worried.

NOEL: Aren't we worried?

JEREMY: Yes. But they don't have to know.

NOEL: Shouldn't Harry be in on this?

JEREMY: Harry is trying to reach headquarters on another matter.

NOEL: What other matter?

JEREMY: We got a transcript of our friends' office conversation this morning. They're talking about a rather disturbing cable Mikhail wants sent to Andropov.

NOEL: Was it about me?

JEREMY: No, not *you*. My stars. It's about Raven.

NOEL: Raven?

JEREMY: Yes. Raven turns out to be their mole in some terrorist organization. ...It's really a bad time for all of D C to be incommunicado.

NOEL: Can't Harry get through?

JEREMY: No. There's a fuss about something coming out tomorrow in the *Post*. It's causing quite a stir. A lot of shredding, apparently. *(Pause, he pours wine, smiles.)* So. What is he like? The elusive Mikhail.

NOEL: *(Unprepared)* He's very *Soviet.*

JEREMY: Any sense of material longings?

NOEL: No. Yes! Yes, there was a ring; he bought her some dinky ring, that we all had to go on and on about. ...His art thing is strong. Almost mystical.

JEREMY: Interesting. Maybe he'd like to *own* art.

NOEL: Maybe.

(They pause. JEREMY *smiles.)*

JEREMY: *(Quietly)* How did it feel?

NOEL: *(The real goods)* It was like...jumping off a cliff.

JEREMY: Did you...sweat?

NOEL: I didn't even notice. My hands were dry, but when I got back to our room, I could wring out my undershirt.

JEREMY: There's nothing like it. ...So. Aside from this telephone number debacle, this was a major success for you.

NOEL: Nobody's going to see it like that.

JEREMY: Well, that all depends on how we write it up. Let me see what you've got so far.

*(*JEREMY *glances at Noel's report.)*

JEREMY: No, *save* it. Put the slip up at the end.

NOEL: But this is when it happened. It was *before* the chess game.

JEREMY: Timing, my boy. Put it at the end of the report. We'll figure out the wording when we get there.

(Enter SYLVIA.*)*

SYLVIA: Noel?

NOEL: Hon—

SYLVIA: Jeremy, I know Noel's career is over and he'll have to retire from the company, get a new job somewhere in America, in a hospital maybe; everybody makes mistakes, you have to get on with your life.

JEREMY: There's no ruined career here.

NOEL: Hon, please—

JEREMY: It's a little *mistake.* We have people on staff that it's their whole job to figure out messes like this. Don't you worry about Noel's job.

(HARRY *enters with transcript.)*

HARRY: I can't get through. It's like all of D C is under water.

JEREMY: Keep trying.

HARRY: They're not even answering *phones.*

SYLVIA: Are you calling them about us?

HARRY: *(Incredulous)* You? No. *(To* JEREMY*)* Is it okay she knows?

(JEREMY *nods.)*

HARRY: We got a transcript that says there's going to be a hit on the Israeli Olympic team.

SYLVIA: It *says* that?

HARRY: Yeah, that's what it *says.* But who knows? They might be trying to fake us out about Raven.

SYLVIA: What's Raven?

HARRY: He's their guy in something called Black September. If we believe this.

NOEL: What are we doing?

HARRY: I'm trying to reach H Q. I've been trying all day.

SYLVIA: No, let's *call* them!

JEREMY: Call who?

SYLVIA: The Israelis. I'm sure they're listed.

HARRY: I sent the cable; that's all I can do.

SYLVIA: Why are we talking about this? Call them up. Warn them.

NOEL: It isn't that easy, Hon.

JEREMY: There are other things to consider.

SYLVIA: What's more important than an Olympic team?

HARRY: It could be a trick to find out if their office is bugged. Which it is.

SYLVIA: Why do you even have their office bugged if it isn't to save Olympic teams?

NOEL: Hon, sit down.

SYLVIA: I want to go home.

JEREMY: Sylvia, please. You're not thinking, you're panicking. *(Pours wine)* Moments like this, you must be steady, fit, calm. Breathe. If you're feeling insecure or uncertain you must come to me. I have a lot more experience. Think of me as your advisor. *(He hands* SYLVIA *wine.)*

SYLVIA: My what?

JEREMY: Your advisor. Your *confidant.*

NOEL: *(Panic)* What's in that glass?!

JEREMY: It's wine.

NOEL: *(Panic)* Then why it is so dark?!

JEREMY: It's a *port.*

NOEL: Oh, okay.

*(*SYLVIA *stares at wine glass in her hand.)*

SYLVIA: *(Realizes)* It was Ay.

JEREMY: What was?

SYLVIA: Ay killed him. His advisor. I have to go.

HARRY: Killed who?

SYLVIA: I have to get back. I have to tell him.

HARRY: Sit down, Sylvia. Nobody's telling anybody anything.

*(*SYLVIA *tries to depart.* NOEL *holds her to prevent her from leaving, almost an embrace. The big phone rings, it sounds very loud, hollow.* JEREMY *picks it up.)*

JEREMY: Yes? Hello, Mary, I'm very busy—what is it— *(Exhales deeply, as* MARY *tells him the news.)* I'll call you— *(Brief pause)* Mary! Don't be ridiculous. We didn't have anything to do with it—I'll talk to you later. *(Hangs up.)*

HARRY: *(To* JEREMY, *about the phone call)* What? Did they—?

JEREMY: Yes. They did.

HARRY: *(Sad)* Oh, man, oh no, oh geez.

SYLVIA: *(Same time)* No, please no—

NOEL: *(Very gently)* Sylvia, Sylvia please—

SYLVIA: Oh. Listen. When you say my name like that I can hear the "Y". *(To the others, very sad)* You could have called them up. You could have called them right away.

HARRY: We don't have that kind of authorization.

SYLVIA: I would have called them.

HARRY: Yeah, and you gave the Soviets your telephone number. Brilliant.

NOEL: She had nothing to do with it.

HARRY: Oh, yeah, right.

JEREMY: Alright now—we'll talk about this later.

SYLVIA: *(She puts down glass.)* I'd like to go, please.

JEREMY: Alright, Dear. No more worries about Noel's career, now.

SYLVIA: No?

JEREMY: He'll be fine; I'll see to it.

SYLVIA: *(Defiant)* I'm the Sylvia with a "Y".

JEREMY: Pardon me?

SYLVIA: Not an "*I*".

*(*SYLVIA *exits.)*

JEREMY: Noel—?

NOEL: She's okay.

JEREMY: Taking this a little hard, isn't she?

HARRY: Well, you know, I don't feel so great myself.

NOEL: Maybe it's because she's ...I don't know. She'll be okay.

Scene Nine

(The apartment. SYLVIA *and* TUT*, looking at his palm. The telephone,* Der Spiegel.*)*

SYLVIA: *(His palm)* See! See this fatty part?! Just like me. You keep things too close to the chest.

TUT: Does it say who killed me?

SYLVIA: That's what I'm saying. It was your own stupid fault.

TUT: *(Sad)* It was my wife, right?

SYLVIA: No, you idiot. Your wife knew you were going to retire.
She wouldn't have done it. She loved you.

TUT: She did?

SYLVIA: But your advisor didn't know you were going to retire, did he?

TUT: No, only me and my wife. It was our secret.

SYLVIA: It was your advisor killed you.

TUT: Ay killed me?

SYLVIA: Yep. Because of your big secret. He didn't know you were going to retire, so he killed you to get the kingdom.

TUT: Boy, I'm a jerk.

SYLVIA: Yeah, you should have had a big retirement party. That's what I'm going to do.*(She gets* MIKHAIL'*s business card; dials phone.)* Five, three, zero, one, nine, five.

TUT: Are you calling the guests?

SYLVIA: Sort of.

TUT: I'm so tired.

SYLVIA: Yeah, you should go back to sleep.

(While SYLVIA *speaks on the phone,* TUT *kisses her on the head before he slowly departs.)*

SYLVIA: *(To phone)* Hello? Varya? This Suzie is. Remember me? Munich, right. ...I'm fine. No, I'm bad. I really bad am. ...No, I'm not about *Nixon* worried. What *about* Nixon? ...Tapes? What tapes—? ...Oh, Varya if it in the *Post* is, it isn't important, but that's not why I upset am. ...Yeah, the athletes, I should them have saved. ...With a phone call. Now I'm just trying to my marriage save. Listen, Varya, I want to tell you that I you really like. ...You did? I so glad am. I you *really* like no matter what I say. Um. Mikhail's office bugged is. And Suzie and Ned our real names aren't, and Noel doesn't hippies like, and I Jewish am, and Noel doesn't—...He is? ...Well, whaddaya know. ...I truly sorry for all the lies and secrets am. ...No, he shouldn't us call back, we're leaving, moving to America. Noel to medical school going is. You should see if you can get Mischa to enroll in one. Bye. Bye bye.

(Hangs up. SYLVIA *looks in magazine, dials.)*

SYLVIA: Hello, is this *Der Spiegel*? Can I please speak to one of your reporters?

(Enter NOEL.*)*

SYLVIA: *(To phone)* Oh, sorry. Can I to one of your reporters speak, please?

NOEL: What are you doing?

SYLVIA: Oh, hi, Noel. I'm talking to *Der Spiegel.*

NOEL: ...Why are you doing *that*?

SYLVIA: You're going to be so mad. This could be our period of estrangement.

NOEL: ...What?

SYLVIA: The period of estrangement that's in my hand. I hope we get back together.

NOEL: Hon, do you need— *(He gets her a glass of wine.)* We'll find a hospital.

SYLVIA: Yes, so you can do your internship.

NOEL: A few weeks. You'll be good as new.

SYLVIA: I don't want any more wine. Wine doesn't agree with me.

NOEL: Okay, okay, no more wine. Please Hon, please put down the phone.

SYLVIA: So I won't be needing any more pills.

NOEL: Whatever you say. Anything you want.

SYLVIA: I already called Varya.

NOEL: Varya?! Varya who?!

SYLVIA: Varya Russian Varya. She really likes us. I told her Mischa should go to medical school, too.

NOEL: Hon, let go of the phone. Right now.

SYLVIA: No. There's one or two things I have to tell you about me and King Tut.

NOEL: ...Is this about your dissertation?

SYLVIA: *(Shocked)* No, I can't tell my committee; I haven't even told you, yet.

NOEL: Told me what?

SYLVIA: About my mistake with the Egyptian teenager.

NOEL: Okay! *(Enormous patience)* Tell me, tell me now! What about your mistake with the Egyptian teenager?

SYLVIA: At first I thought he was you. Or you were him. But you weren't. You were you. And I love you. I want to love you.

NOEL: *(Gently)* Sylvia—

SYLVIA: Oh!

NOEL: What?

SYLVIA: Say my name again.

NOEL: Sylvia, Hon, dear Sylvia. Please put down the phone. Whatever you've done, we'll fix it.

SYLVIA: I don't want to fix it. It's me or the company.

NOEL: What?!

SYLVIA: Oh, yes. I'm sure that's true now.

(NOEL tries to take the phone.)

NOEL: Hon, give me the phone. Let go of the phone.

SYLVIA: Not until everybody knows everything.

NOEL: Let go. Right now.

SYLVIA: You let go right now.

NOEL: Hon—

SYLVIA: Don't call me Hon; I have a name. And I really like how you say it.

(They hold onto the phone. Lights fade out.)

END OF PLAY

PRONUNCIATION HELP

This German word .... sounds likes this *(Meaning in parenthesis)*

aufwiedersehen .... auf veeder zae un *(Goodbye)*
bin .... rhymes with gin *(Am)*
die .... rhymes with bee *(The)*
der .... rhymes with air *(The)*
das . dahs *(Rhymes with what you say when the doctor looks at your throat)* (The)
dein .... dine *(your)*
ein .... eye + n *(One)*
eine .... eye nuh *(One)*
etwas .... *et (Rhymes with bet)* vas *(Something)*
es .... ess rhymes with Bess *(It)*
ganz .... gantz *(Completely)*
grosse .... *gross*uh *(Big)*
guten abend .... gooten abent *(Good evening)*
Herr .... hair *(Man)*
ich .... somewhere between ick and ish *(I)*
Ja .... ya *(yes)*
jawol .... yavol *(yes)*
kinder .... as in kindergarten *(Children)*
mein .... mine *(My)*
meine .... my *nuh(My)*
sie .... zee, rhymes with bee *(you, they)*
shrei .... shrye, rhymes with cry *(Noise)*
sind .... zint, rhymes with glint *(Are)*
sein .... zine, rhymes with mine *(your, their)*
sehr .... zare, rhymes with air *(Very)*
Spiegel .... *shpeegul (Mirror)*
tag .... taahk *(Day)*
und .... oont *(And)*
wir .... veer, rhymes with deer *(We)*

Russian Names

Ivan .... Ee*van*
Mikhail .... Mik *Kyle*
Varya .... *Var*ya

GERALD'S GOOD IDEA

ACKNOWLEDGMENTS

For support with the development of GERALD'S GOOD IDEA, thanks to New Dramatists in N Y C; The New Play Center in Vancouver, B C; The Sundance Institute, Utah; The Mark Taper Forum, Los Angeles; New York Theater Workshop; and King County Arts Commission in Washington State. In addition to the institutional support, many actors helped, some of them again and again.

for Chris McCann

CHARACTERS

GLADYS: *black*
SYLVIA: *black. Has an advantage and is able to put things together fast, but she is always trying to work it out and doesn't know everything in advance.*
GERALD: *white*
SIMONE: *white*
ELAINE: *white*
BOBBY: *white*
WAYNE: *black*
STANLEY: *black*
LOUISE: *black*
FRANCIS: *white*

All characters are between thirty-five and forty-five years-old.

None of these characters smoke. None of these characters end their sentences up? As if they were asking questions? When there is nary a question to be found?

ACT ONE

Scene One

*(*SYLVIA *sits at a table on a cloud. She wears rags.* GLADYS *enters wearing a maid's uniform and carrying high heels.* GLADYS *sits.)*

SYLVIA: Nice dress.

GLADYS: It's a maid's uniform!

SYLVIA: Just say "thank you."

GLADYS: I'm not feeling particularly grateful!

SYLVIA: Thank you is always the best reply to a compliment.

GLADYS: How come you're wearing those rags?

SYLVIA: If you say something besides thank you, something like "oh, do you really like it?" Or, "You look nice, too—"

GLADYS: I wasn't going to say—

SYLVIA: Then I have to *respond*. Whereas, "thank you" puts an end to the whole thing. Any other reply, *any* other reply, and we're deep into it.

GLADYS: ...I'll remember.

(Brief pause)

SYLVIA: Nice dress.

GLADYS: Thank you!

SYLVIA: What are those? *(Points to shoes)*

GLADYS: High heels.

SYLVIA: What are you going to do with them?

GLADYS: They're shoes.

SYLVIA: But you're not wearing them.

GLADYS: I'll wear them, okay? *(Puts them on.)* Ouch ouch ouch.

SYLVIA: Oh, I see, I *see.*

*(*GLADYS *removes shoes, picks up menu.)*

GLADYS: Is somebody coming for our order?

SYLVIA: No one is coming.

GLADYS: I always get this. *(Points in the menu)*

SYLVIA: What about one of *these*? *(Points)*

GLADYS: Fattening!

SYLVIA: You *never* had one of these?

GLADYS: They make you fat.

SYLVIA: *(Points)* What about this?

GLADYS: That's *raw*. They don't cook that. You catch stuff if you eat that.

SYLVIA: What *did* you eat?

GLADYS: This, *this*, I told you, I ate this.

SYLVIA: What's in it?

GLADYS: Lettuce. It's mostly lettuce. Let's not discuss it anymore, alright? *(A pause. She looks around.)* Isn't there anything else? T V, or something.

SYLVIA: T V? Well, there's....

(A T V appears.)

GLADYS: Oh, a movie! *(Deep relief)* Great, great.

SYLVIA: This isn't a movie; this is a real life.

GLADYS: Are those ant hills?

SYLVIA: ... People hills.

GLADYS: I love special effects. ...That raggedy woman...she looks familiar. I've seen her.

SYLVIA: *(Sarcastic)* Recently?

GLADYS: Yes. I saw her in something recently. What's in the pouch?

SYLVIA: A baby.

GLADYS: Have you seen this before?

SYLVIA: Oh, yes.

GLADYS: What's the man doing?

SYLVIA: Looking for food.

GLADYS: Look at the air! Looks sort of—sticky. It's all...why is the air that color? When is this?

SYLVIA: Many years into the future.

GLADYS: *(Watches intently)* The man's dizzy. Yep, he's going down—kerplop. He looks dead. There she goes; she'll never find him. She shouldn't take the baby. *(Watches, reacts)* Yuk yuckity yuk. I wouldn't go up to *my* waist in that gooey...yellow...whatever-it-is.

SYLVIA: Water.

GLADYS: Oh good, she's pulling herself out. Oh no! It's alive, it's alive!

SYLVIA: Snake.

GLADYS: I thought it was a branch.

SYLVIA: So did I.

GLADYS: *(Watches, shouts at T V)* Hey! Hey! Don't go down there. Don't go down there! Why's she taking the baby into that steaming pit?

SYLVIA: She's looking for drinking water.

GLADYS: I wouldn't go down there for *champagne. (Happy)* Oh, look, look! There he is; she's almost there. *(Shouts at T V)* Hey! Hey! He's across the bog, just across the bog. Go get him, go on girl, go on! *(Film ends)* What happened? What happened to the reception?

SYLVIA: There isn't any more.

GLADYS: What? You showed me an incomplete movie? An unfinished film? I want to see the end of that movie.

SYLVIA: That was the end.

GLADYS: A bit abrupt, don't you think?

SYLVIA: Yes, I do.

GLADYS: That's a very unsatisfying end. I'd prefer to see a better end.

SYLVIA: Personally, I'm hoping the whole thing can be reworked.

GLADYS: That woman? Really cool. Sees what has to be done, does it. Doesn't matter what's in the way. Bogs, slime, snakes, just goes ahead and does it. You know, you have to be like that in life, just to rise to the challenges of everyday existence. Now, I didn't have bogs or stuff, but I, you know, I rose to the occasion. I think I lived a lot like that lady. A lot. Like her.

*(*SYLVIA *stares at* GLADYS, GLADYS *fidgets.)*

GLADYS: So! You ever want to go back? *(Looks at* SYLVIA*'s rags)* Oh! I guess you wouldn't want to go back. I guess it was pretty raggedy for you.

SYLVIA: Pretty raggedy.

GLADYS: Yeah, it was raggedy for me, too. Sitting alone through the night.

SYLVIA: Staying alive through the night.

GLADYS: Dieting.

SYLVIA: Scavenging.

GLADYS: Boys.

SYLVIA: Gangs.

GLADYS: White people.

SYLVIA: No white people.

GLADYS: ...Pardon me?

SYLVIA: No white people.

GLADYS: What do you mean no white people?

SYLVIA: There were no white people.

GLADYS: Aren't we from the same time?

SYLVIA: No. My time is much later.

GLADYS: Wow. No white people.

SYLVIA: And that isn't all.

GLADYS: You didn't know any white people? White people, let me tell you about white people. You're standing there, you're next in line to get waited on, the sales person, the *white* sales person, she walks up to the white person who is standing in line *behind* you because she can't even *see* you. And when they *do* see you, *If* they do see you, if they *talk* to you, they get a southern accent. And then they get English-brain-drain and completely lose their syntax and talk to you in unintelligible fragments. You should go back. Check out white people.

SYLVIA: I've seen them.

GLADYS: Where have you seen them? You haven't seen them. There weren't any white people in that movie.

SYLVIA: True, but there are white people in this. *(She snaps at T V.)*

GLADYS: *(Watches, rooted)* That was...

SYLVIA: Your life.

GLADYS: That wasn't all of it.

SYLVIA: That was all of it.

GLADYS: Noooo. What about the time I—

SYLVIA: That was there.

GLADYS: I didn't see it.

SYLVIA: You better watch again. *(Snaps)* See it that time?

GLADYS: Yes. What about the—

SYLVIA: They were there.

GLADYS: I don't think so.

SYLVIA: Sure, here. *(Snaps)* See them that time?

GLADYS: What about my—

SYLVIA: That was just an *idea*. You never actually *did* that. Let's watch it again.

GLADYS: *(Fast)* No, no that's fine.

SYLVIA: No, let's watch it again! *(Snaps)*

GLADYS: No! *(Short pains)* Ah, ee, oh, ah. *(Pause, breath)*

(SYLVIA snaps.)

GLADYS: *(Short pains)* Ah, ee, oh, ah. Will you please stop that?

(SYLVIA snaps.)

GLADYS: *(Snaps at the T V)* Stop it, stop it, ah, ee, oh, ah. *(Breath)* That's enough, that's enough, don't do that anymore. Put on the other one.

SYLVIA: Not until it's reworked.

GLADYS: Fine! Just don't put me on again.

SYLVIA: You could read the menu. Or...you could watch again. *(Snaps)*

GLADYS: No, no! Ah, ee, oh, ah. *(Breath)* Give me the menu. *(Reads menu)* I never had one of these, I never *dared* have one of these, One of these was on the table once and I *turned it down*! I can't read this. *(Puts down menu, the movie starts)* Ah ee oh ah. Ah ee oh ah. Ah, ee, oh, I...I...I gotta, I gotta, help! I gotta go back!

(The T V snaps off. A staircase appears.)

GLADYS: *(Scared)* Oh.

SYLVIA: Don't forget your tall shoes.

GLADYS: *High* shoes. Um. Goodbye. I'll be seeing ya.

(GLADYS exits. SYLVIA stands up and walks on tiptoe, as if walking in high heels.)

SYLVIA: Ouch ouch ouch.

Scene Two

(The living room of the amazing apartment of SIMONE and GERALD. They are rich.)

GERALD: Did you get...um...?

SIMONE: What? Did I get what?

GERALD: That nice cheese. Did you have a chance to get that nice cheese?

SIMONE: I didn't go downtown.

GERALD: Too bad! That's a nice cheese. Damn. The bar looks good, though. Don't you think?

SIMONE: It's fine.

GERALD: No, it's really good. Did you see it? I put out the good stuff. Do you think that's a good idea?

SIMONE: It's what we always do. *(She lies on the floor.)*

GERALD: Then it's a good idea. This bar looks *good*. It's a fine line between generosity and ostentatiousness. Don't you think?

SIMONE: I don't know.

GERALD: What are you—?

SIMONE: I'm exhausted.

GERALD: Well, the place looks great.

SIMONE: Don't thank me, I watched T V all day.

GERALD: Why did you do that?

SIMONE: So I didn't have to think.

GERALD: Did it work?

SIMONE: No. I thought about how how disgusting I am.

GERALD: Why didn't you just...turn it off?

SIMONE: If I move from the bed, I am going to have to *decide* what else to do and I can't *decide* what else to do. I'm melting.

GERALD: Do you think I should make a pitcher of something? Daiquiris maybe? Daiquiris are so fey. Maybe I should make a pitcher of martinis. *(He does.)*

SIMONE: I'm a pig.

GERALD: Don't say pig.

SIMONE: Pig. Pig.

GERALD: *(Bolstering her)* If you had gone downtown and gotten that nice cheese, you wouldn't feel this way.

SIMONE: If you had told me to go downtown to get it, I would have gone downtown to get it.

GERALD: I did tell you.

SIMONE: You didn't.

GERALD: Right before we fell asleep. Remember? I kissed your neck and said, get that nice cheese for tomorrow night. You said, mmm hum.

SIMONE: ...You should have told me again, *today*. You should have *reminded* me. You *should* have.

GERALD: You're sure I should have?

SIMONE: Of course I'm sure.

GERALD: *(Happy)* Well, Simone, that's pretty decisive. I mean, you seem decisive enough now.

SIMONE: Now, sure, now I do.

GERALD: Why not before?

SIMONE: Before was during the *day*. Now is *night*. I'm decisive at night. Just fine. The daylight confounds me.

GERALD: ...I don't understand.

SIMONE: Of course you don't understand. You only see me at night. At night all things are possible because you won't start them until tomorrow. Then, when it is tomorrow, and it's *day*, it's all too confounding.

GERALD: I see you on weekends.

SIMONE: Same as night.

GERALD: No.

SIMONE: Yes. Because on the weekend you won't *start* anything until *Monday*. I'm useless.

GERALD: You're not! Don't say that. I...couldn't get through a single day without your help. And if you had gone downtown, and gotten that nice cheese, you'd feel...great!

SIMONE: I'm melting away.

GERALD: *(At a table)* Here it is!

SIMONE: What?

GERALD: The cheese. This is the nice cheese I wanted you to get.

GLADYS: *(Off)* I got the cheese.

GERALD: Oh. *(Shouting)* Come here a second, Gladys!

(GLADYS enters looking around.)

GERALD: Thank you for getting the cheese, Gladys.

GLADYS: *(Embarrassed)* Oh, I...

GERALD: No, it was very thoughtful.

SIMONE: Gladys...?

GLADYS: Yes?

SIMONE: How do I look?

GLADYS: Nice. *(Awed)* Look at this room. Everything is so...nice.

SIMONE: ...Thank you.

GERALD: Yes, thank you, Gladys. *(Brief silence.)* Bye bye.

GLADYS: Oh, right. *(Can't quite leave the room)*

GERALD: Gladys, do you want....

GLADYS: Fine, I'm fine. I'm leaving.*(Exits)*

GERALD: You could have asked *me* how you look.

SIMONE: How do I look?

GERALD: You might have mentioned that Gladys got the cheese.

SIMONE: How do I look?

GERALD: Did I tell her to get it?

SIMONE: Look look look.

GERALD: Oh, well. This is great. This is going to be so great. *(A little dance)* Did you tell everybody we were having a surprise?

SIMONE: Yes!

GERALD: And you called her? That Sylvia woman?

SIMONE: Sure.

GERALD: And she's coming?

SIMONE: Yes, she's coming—we're having the party, aren't we?

GERALD: You're amazing.

SIMONE: I'm melting.

GERALD: This is going to be so...great! Great, great.

SIMONE: It's just a party, Gerald.

GERALD: It's a Gerald Party, and a Gerald Party is never just a party. How much does she charge?

SIMONE: I don't know. I gave her the Visa number.

GERALD: She took a credit card number?

SIMONE: ...Well, yes, I think she did.

GERALD: I suppose it's all right. Did you make the list?

SIMONE: Yes, I made the list!

GERALD: This is going to be the most amazing thing we've ever done.

SIMONE: I'm not up to the most amazing thing we've ever done.

GERALD: *(Hugs* SIMONE*)* Yes, you are. You rise to every occasion. Simone always comes through for Little Gerald.

(Doorbell)

GERALD: Hooray.

*(*GERALD *answers the door.* SYLVIA *stands in doorway.* GERALD *does not see her.)*

GERALD: There's nobody there. That's funny...

SYLVIA: You really *don't* see black people. Oh! I forgot. *(She makes herself visible.)*

GERALD: I could have sworn—Ahhhhh! I'm sorry, I didn't.... My goodness! *(A breath)* Can I help you?

SYLVIA: I'm Sylvia.

GERALD: I beg your pardon?

SYLVIA: Sylvia. I'm expected.

GERALD: *You're* Sylvia?

SYLVIA: Yes. I am.

GERALD: Oh. Hello! We're expecting you.

SYLVIA: I know.

GERALD: How are you?

SYLVIA: *(Still in doorway)* Fine. You?

GERALD: Uh, fine. Darling, this is Sylvia. She's expected.

SIMONE: I know. Hi.

SYLVIA: How do you do?

SIMONE: Okay.

SYLVIA: ...Can I...come in?

GERALD: Of course, of course. Come in, come in. Yes, yes, come in, please. Darling, this is Sylvia. This is my wife.

SIMONE: Hi, again.

GLADYS: *(Entering)* Ahhhhhh.

SYLVIA: Hello. I'm Sylvia. I'm expected.

GLADYS: Not by me!

GERALD: Gladys, did you want—?

GLADYS: Coat. I'm here to hang up the coat. But, I see there isn't one. So, I'll...depart. *(Exits)*

SYLVIA: Was that the person who called me?

SIMONE: ...I called you.

SYLVIA: No.

SIMONE: Me.

SYLVIA: On the phone, I got...a picture ... not of you.

SIMONE: Well. It was me. Simone.

SYLVIA: Simone?

SIMONE: Yes, Simone. That's my name.

SYLVIA: I don't think so.

SIMONE: What do you mean?

GERALD: You're right! Simone changed her name. It used to be Dorothy.

SYLVIA: Well, you're well rid of that.

GERALD: I quite agree.

SIMONE: You're supposed to tell secrets, but not my ones.

SYLVIA: Things pop out of my mouth.

GERALD: No. No, no. We can't have indiscriminate popping. You'll have to have more control over it than that.

SYLVIA: I don't have more control over it than that.

SIMONE: Let's call it off.

SYLVIA: *(Worried)* Oh. Of course, if that's your choice. I can't, however, refund your money until I get paid by American Express.

GERALD: *(To* SIMONE*)* I thought you said Visa.

SIMONE: ...I um...I don't know.

SYLVIA: American Express. 33377893625095.

GERALD: *(Pause)* Is that my American...?

*(*SYLVIA *nods.)*

GERALD: ...I usually don't give out my credit card number over the phone. There's—

SYLVIA: —a lot of fraud.

GERALD: Yes, a person—

SYLVIA: —can't be too careful.

GERALD: That's what I think...I get very nervous when I have to give out my credit card number on the phone.

SYLVIA: You should see a doctor about that. I love the whole promissory notion of credit. The vacuum you promise to later fill. The trust; that's the most important thing, the trust.

GERALD: I don't know.

SYLVIA: I do. Trust me.

SIMONE: I don't want Francis to find out my name is Dorothy.

GERALD: Francis doesn't gossip.

SIMONE: Everywhere I go, "Is that a Dorothy *dress* or a Simone *gown*?"

SYLVIA: Could I wash someplace?

SIMONE: "Pardon me dear, was that Simone speaking, or is Dorothy rearing her ugly head?"

GERALD: Down the hall on the left.

SYLVIA: Thank you. It's very dirty down here. *(Exits)*

GERALD: Down where?

SIMONE: Maybe she's from Connecticut.

GERALD: You didn't tell me she was black.

SIMONE: I never saw her.

GERALD: Couldn't you tell on the phone?

SIMONE: How do you do that?

GERALD: She has my American Express card number. Memorized.

SIMONE: People will wave to me across crowded living rooms and shout, "Hello, Dotty." ...I need some chips.

GERALD: No, you don't. You don't need chips.

SIMONE: I'm going out for chips. I'm a pig.

GERALD: Stop saying that! I did not marry a pig.

SIMONE: Let's ask her to leave.

GERALD: You constantly belittle yourself. You are an asset to me.

SIMONE: If she goes away, I won't need chips.

GERALD: You have my shirts laundered, you take care of my social calendar, you decorate. You do all of our finances.

SIMONE: Oh...

GERALD: You remember what everybody drinks. Those might be small things, but my life is too complicated for just one person. You are very valuable.

(SYLVIA *re-enters.)*

SYLVIA: Your water is so clear.

GERALD: Thank you.

SYLVIA: There was perfume. I dabbed it on.

GERALD: *(cheery)* That's what it's for.

SIMONE: I have to go out.

(GLADYS *enters and gets* SIMONE's *fur coat from the closet.)*

SYLVIA: *(To* SIMONE*)* For chips?

GERALD: You overheard that.

SIMONE: Stop that! I mean, please, if you can, stop it. I don't want to be a part of the party games. I don't want anybody to know I get up in the middle of the night for chips.

SYLVIA: I used to wake up hungry in the middle of the night.

GERALD: How did you stop?

SYLVIA: I died.

SIMONE: I'll bring some back for you, too.

GERALD: Don't go out for chips.

SIMONE: *(Putting on fur coat)* There are worse things, Gerald. I am not up for this party.

GLADYS: *(To* SIMONE*)* Laundry room.

(SIMONE *exits.* GLADYS *exits to the kitchen.)*

SYLVIA: Simone is not up for this party.

GERALD: I hope she comes back.

SYLVIA: She'll be back. *(Eating)* Nice cheese.

GERALD: *(Proudly)* I know.

SYLVIA: *(Excited)* Nice. It's so *nice*. It's a nice cheese.

GERALD: Thank you. I'm sorry Simone left.

SYLVIA: She's quite beautiful.

GERALD: *(Happy)* Do you think so?

SYLVIA: Yes. And so white.

GERALD: Yes, *quite* ...pretty.

SYLVIA: Pink, actually.

GERALD: ...Simone is...very rosy.

SYLVIA: Yes, that's the word. Rosy. Nice.

GERALD: Hard to see, sometimes. Time...you know.

SYLVIA: You only see the potato-chip crumbs.

GERALD: ...So! Would you like to know who's coming?

SYLVIA: Yes, get me the list. It's in the bedroom.

(GERALD exits. GLADYS enters.)

GLADYS: What are you doing in *my* movie?

SYLVIA: I need it to go well.

GLADYS: You might have changed your clothes.

SYLVIA: No one will notice my clothes. Look at this place! Why is that lady so scared?

GLADYS: She'll calm down when she finds the chips.

SYLVIA: She must eat a lot of chips.

GLADYS: Did you eat something yet?

SYLVIA: Of course. Have you?

GLADYS: No.

(They stare at cheese. SYLVIA eats some.)

SYLVIA: Ummm. You should try it.

GLADYS: *(Tries cheese)* Oh, oh. This is really good. Oh, my. No wonder he wanted me to get it.

SYLVIA: He wanted Simone to get it.

GLADYS: I meant that, I meant no wonder he wanted Simone to get it.

GERALD: *(Off)* I can't find the list.

SYLVIA: *(Shouting)* On the night stand. That was *you* who called, not Simone.

GLADYS: Yeah, and if I'd known it was *you* I'd have hung up!

SYLVIA: Does he know you make her calls?

GLADYS: You mean G-G-G-...?

SYLVIA: Spit it out.

GLADYS: The man, the guy...G-G-...

SYLVIA: Gerald.

GLADYS: Thank you. It's very complicated. I make her calls; she stands next to me.

SYLVIA: And you tell her what the other person says.

GLADYS: Well, sure. Except today. I didn't tell her anything. Today there are going to be some *real* surprises.

SYLVIA: Yes, I looked it up. Today could be a very important day.

GLADYS: This isn't going to be the day it was!

SYLVIA: That's important.

*(*GERALD *enters.)*

GERALD: Here's the list. *(Mistakes* GLADYS *for* SIMONE*)* Simone! You're back! *(He hugs* GLADYS.*)* See, you didn't need those greasy little chips.

GLADYS: *(Shocked)* G-G-G-...

GERALD: *(Stunned)* I'm sorry, I...

GLADYS: I—I—

GERALD: I'm sorry, I...I thought you were Simone.

GLADYS: Well, that's all the explanation I need. I'll just retire to the kitchen... *(Backs up.)*

SYLVIA: That way.

*(*GLADYS *exits.)*

GERALD: *(Forcing a laugh)* I could have sworn she was...

SYLVIA: A perfectly natural mistake. Does she have a name?

GERALD: Of course. What would you like to know about the guests?

SYLVIA: ...Nothing.

GERALD: I thought, you'd want to know things about the guests.

SYLVIA: No.

GERALD: I thought I might be able to help. Make things...hop. You know.

SYLVIA: Things will hop.

GERALD: But I got the list for you. *(Reading)* Gerald, that's me. Simone you met, Francis, Bobby and Elaine. Here.

SYLVIA: This is a very short list. *(Keeps list)*

GERALD: Well. I thought I'd—

SYLVIA: Try me out; see how it went; then have me over for the big party.

GERALD: Well, I have a reputation. I mean, I am—

SYLVIA: Known for my parties.

GERALD: And it isn't because I risk things. These people, well, they—

SYLVIA: Don't matter.

GERALD: ...don't matter. Um...Want to tell me how you ...do it? It is just tricks, isn't it?

SYLVIA: It's hunches.

GERALD: The brochure said you could alter the future.

SYLVIA: The past.

GERALD: It was very nice.

SYLVIA: Thank you.

GERALD: Five color, plus tints. Very professional.

SYLVIA: Thank you.

GERALD: I could use a printer like that. Where'd you have them done?

SYLVIA: It. Not them, it. I just had one done.

GERALD: ...Well, it's very nice. So. ...Hunches.

(Doorbell)

GERALD: I know that ring! Simone's back.

SYLVIA: I don't think so. Just a hunch.

GERALD: Oh, hello. Hello. This is Sylvia, Bobby, Elaine.

(Enter BOBBY *and* ELAINE. GLADYS *enters, hangs coats, exits.)*

BOBBY: Hello, Gerald. Where's my girl? *(To* SYLVIA*)* Hi! Who are you?

SYLVIA: Sylvia.

BOBBY: Hi, Sylvia. You a friend of somebody?

SYLVIA: I hope so.

BOBBY: I mean somebody here.

SYLVIA: Not yet.

ELAINE: Where *is* Simone?

GERALD: She's gone out for some last-minute preparations.

ELAINE: Chips?!

SYLVIA: That's what she said.

BOBBY: Simone is so cute when she eats chips.

ELAINE: That's not what you say when I eat chips.

BOBBY: In the middle of the night? Crumbs in the bed?

ELAINE: Where's our surprise, Gerald?

BOBBY: I thought maybe Simone painted the place black, again. *(To* SYLVIA*)* Oh, sorry.

SYLVIA: You eat chips, too?

ELAINE: Yeah. But I do other things.

SYLVIA: What?

ELAINE: Well. I'm Bobby's wife.

BOBBY: *(Coaching)* Now, Elaine, remember...?

ELAINE: Right. I am a person in my own right.

SYLVIA: *(To* ELAINE*)* What do you do?

ELAINE: ...Bobby's a writer.

SYLVIA: What do *you* do?

ELAINE: Bobby's a great writer.

GERALD: Francis will confirm that when he gets here.

BOBBY: I didn't know Francis was coming.

GERALD: He's coming. You should make another pitch, Bobby.

ELAINE: Gerald, can I make the drinks?

GERALD: *(Smile)* Caught in the act of neglecting my guests. I'm such a rotten host.

BOBBY: You are when it's family.

GERALD: I beg your pardon.

BOBBY: You hop-to when it's the Vice President and Mrs Somebody-or-Other. Or Francis.

ELAINE: *(At bar)* What would you like, Sylvia?

GERALD: I'll do that.

ELAINE: Aw.

GERALD: What would you like, Sylvia? We're fully stocked, the best of everything. Martinis. Boodles, very dry.

SYLVIA: Let me see...

GERALD: Take your time. You shouldn't rush when you're about to sip perfection.

SYLVIA: I think I'll have ...water.

GERALD: We have everything.

SYLVIA: Water.

GERALD: Now really—

SYLVIA: A water. A big one.

GERALD: Okay. *(Making it)* A double water. Bobby? Martini?

BOBBY: Water.

GERALD: Fine, water. Martini, Elaine?

ELAINE: Oh, I'll have a Tab.

GERALD: *(Between his teeth)* Tab, fine. Here. And I'll have a scotch. If nobody objects.

ELAINE: Why should anybody object?

GERALD: ...What are you working on these days, Bob?

BOBBY: I'm dialogue gathering. Today I see these two Latinish girls walking down the street and one of them is crying death tears.

ELAINE: Death tears? Death tears? What are death tears? There you go. There you go.

BOBBY: Tears you cry when somebody dies.

ELAINE: Bobby! Nobody knows that. How's a person supposed to know that? You made that up. You didn't read it. You didn't hear it on the television. You made it up.

BOBBY: Can't a guy have an original thought?

ELAINE: How's a person supposed to understand him when he makes things up?

BOBBY: I thought she was crying over something really big. A big massacre. I mean everybody's got relatives in Latin America, right? And this girl is crying death tears. So I perk up. I'm gonna hear some real dialogue, full of pain and loss. And I listen. The not-crying girl says to the crying girl, "You can't let him do this to you. You can't let him do this to you." It was just a guy. She was crying death tears over some guy.

ELAINE: Did you write it down?

BOBBY: I didn't bother.

ELAINE: The whole country, the whole world gathers dialogue about love, and you don't think it's important enough to write it down?

BOBBY: There's enough people writing about love. I don't have to.

ELAINE: And they're making a living.

GERALD: Cheese? Elaine, Bob?

BOBBY: I make a living.

ELAINE: Ha.

BOBBY: I make a living. We're not on welfare.

ELAINE: You're not on television.

BOBBY: I don't write for television.

ELAINE: It's just like Gerald says.

BOBBY: ...What Gerald says? What, pray tell, does Gerald say?

GERALD: Oh, now...

ELAINE: "Bobby's afraid to lower his standards. He's not good enough to write *great* stuff, and he's *too* good to write for the nintey-eight percent of the country that watches television. The stuff Bobby writes the ninety-eight percent can't understand. And the other two percent aren't interested because he's not *that* good. He's just good enough to be a complete failure."

BOBBY: *(Sarcastic)* Well, Gerald knows a whole lot about writing.

ELAINE: Francis said it too.

BOBBY: Word for word?

ELAINE: *(Suspicious.)* What?

BOBBY: Did Francis repeat it word for word?

ELAINE: What are you talking about?

BOBBY: I'm just trying to get a picture of the event. Was Francis standing there when Gerald said it? Did Francis then repeat it word for word in case you missed something? Did the two of them have this simultaneous thought while separated by miles of hills and dales? How did this come to pass—that Gerald said this highly insulting thing about me, and Francis repeated it?

ELAINE: It isn't insulting. You didn't mean it to be insulting.

GERALD: No, no, not a bit.

BOBBY: *(To GERALD)* I should pitch my work to a guy who thinks I'm a snob?

SYLVIA: *(To GERALD)* How *did* you mean it?

GERALD: Pardon?

SYLVIA: If you didn't mean it as an insult, how did you mean it?

GERALD: Actually...as a compliment.

BOBBY: I'm gonna go look for Simone.

(GLADYS enters, gets BOBBY's coat.)

ELAINE: She'll be back.

BOBBY: Well, then I'll see her back here. Meanwhile, I'll be looking for her, out there.

ELAINE: I don't want you to write for television.

BOBBY: No?

ELAINE: No. But I don't think it would hurt to maybe write about love.

BOBBY: I'll think about it.

ELAINE: Okay. Don't slam the door.

BOBBY: I wasn't *going* to, Elaine.

ELAINE: Okay. Will you be back?

BOBBY: Yes.

ELAINE: Okay.

GLADYS: *(To BOBBY)* Laundry room.

(BOBBY exits. GLADYS exits to kitchen.)

ELAINE: I am so stupid. How could I be this stupid?

GERALD: Study?

ELAINE: I hope he comes back.

SYLVIA: He'll be back.

GERALD: Drink, Elaine?

ELAINE: No. You know, he could make a lot of money. Francis said. Right, Gerald?

GERALD: That's true. *(Fixes himself another drink)*

ELAINE: But he won't write for television.

SYLVIA: What *does* he write?

ELAINE: Directions. Instructions. How-to? You know, "Wet hair, apply shampoo, lather. Rinse, repeat." *(Proudly)* Bobby wrote that. He could make big money if he wrote for television. But he won't.

SYLVIA: That upsets you?

ELAINE: Yeah.

SYLVIA: Why?

ELAINE: I'm just, you know, tired.

SYLVIA: Sure. I know tired. So how about the dogs?

ELAINE: Gerald, you told her about the dogs! I told you not to tell.

GERALD: Well...

SYLVIA: You must really love it.

ELAINE: Oh, I do. But Bobby doesn't know about this, okay?

SYLVIA: Why not?

ELAINE: Bobby wouldn't understand this at all.

SYLVIA: He might.

GERALD: Bobby only understands *endangered* species.

ELAINE: Bobby, he understands things that are important. You know, politics, civil rights, high fiber. But dog competitions! He'd just...never, you know?

SYLVIA: Are you going to judge a show soon?

ELAINE: Oh, no, no. I mean, no. You can't just go *judge* a dog show. You have to *study*. It's hard. When you're standing there in a ring and ten Scotties prance through, the first thing you think is "there is absolutely no difference between any of these dogs." And you panic, you know. But, hey, after a minute, two minutes of watching those ten Scotties, they all suddenly identify themselves. Ten little individuals with fur.

SYLVIA: So now you can identify them.

ELAINE: But not fast enough. I mean, there's thousands of people watching you when you do this.

GERALD: Elaine is very good at it.

SYLVIA: You go to the competitions?

ELAINE: Gerald is very supportive.

SYLVIA: I can imagine. You're Simone's sister.

ELAINE: Oh, thank you. Simone's beautiful, isn't she?

SYLVIA: Uh huh.

ELAINE: And thin. I wish I were thin.

SYLVIA: Why?

ELAINE: Why? Are you kidding? *Why*?

SYLVIA: No, I'm not kidding; why?

ELAINE: Gerald, tell her.

GERALD: Don't look at me. I don't know what all this "thin" is about.

ELAINE: Gerald, you do too know what this thin is about. You do ads.

GERALD: Those ads aren't for people I know.

ELAINE: I *want* to be thin, okay? I want it.

SYLVIA: Well, if you *want* it, if you really want it, don't snack at midnight.

ELAINE: I have to. I can't sleep.

SYLVIA: Snack at nine. Then you won't be hungry at bedtime.

ELAINE: You think?

SYLVIA: I know. And pick up your feet.

ELAINE: When I walk?

SYLVIA: You'll use more calories, and you won't trip as much.

ELAINE: Oh, I trip all the time.

SYLVIA: That'll help. Give it six months; you'll be as skinny as Simone.

GERALD: She doesn't want to be as skinny as Simone. Just don't even think of it, Elaine; you have a lovely shape, and just forget it. *(To* SYLVIA*)* What are you doing?

ELAINE: *(Picks up her feet around the room)* She's giving me a hand is all. You know I want to be thin. Bobby wants me to be thin. He always says I should be like Simone.

GERALD: Are you going to do what Bobby wants, or are you going to do what I want?!

ELAINE: Uh. I don't know.

GERALD: Elaine, would you go see if you can find the mustard?

ELAINE: Huh? Uh, sure, sure. *(Exits to kitchen)*

GERALD: You are making me very...She doesn't need to diet.

SYLVIA: Did you always want the wrong sister?

GERALD: Of course not.

SYLVIA: Can't take a fat girl to parties? Is that it?

GERALD: Well, you can...I mean...No...that's not it!

SYLVIA: ...So. You are white people.

GERALD: I *hate* that. I hate it when black people say, "You white people."

SYLVIA: I didn't say, "You white people."

GERALD: You know what's wrong with you people?

SYLVIA: Who "you people?"

GERALD: ...Did I say "you people?"

SYLVIA: You did.

GERALD: I'm sorry. That was...a generalization. And I apologize.

SYLVIA: Okay.

GERALD: ...That was good. That stuff with the dogs. Nobody knows about that. What—? Did you see dog hairs on her? She's always covered with dog hairs.

SYLVIA: I said it and heard it and knew it.

GERALD: That's how I know things.

SYLVIA: No, that's how you *decide* you know things.

GERALD: You think you have an exclusive on this type of experience, well, you don't. You're not the only ones.

SYLVIA: Pardon me, when you say "you" do you mean "me?"

GERALD: I mean black people. You black people aren't the only people who experience extra-psychic things.

SYLVIA: You know a lot of black people?

GERALD: Well, sure, I mean, you know. Around.

SYLVIA: This building, for example, has many black tenants?

GERALD: No. It's a co-op.

SYLVIA: Oh.

GERALD: So they don't...*want* to live here.

SYLVIA: I see.

GERALD: They really don't.

SYLVIA: Uh huh.

GERALD: They could.

SYLVIA: Yes.

GERALD: But, they don't want to.

SYLVIA: So, that works out nicely then.

GERALD: Yes—What do you mean?

*(*ELAINE *reenters.)*

ELAINE: I can't find it.

GERALD: What?!

SYLVIA: The mustard.

GERALD: Did you ask Gladys?

ELAINE: No, I didn't want to interrupt her dance. What do you want it for, anyway?

GERALD: The hors d'oeuvres.

ELAINE: *(Happy)* The ones behind the mayonnaise under the towel on the second shelf?

GERALD: Yes. Those. Why don't you bring them out?

ELAINE: I didn't have one. I'll bring them out.

SYLVIA: You sure get the girls jumping for you.

GERALD: Never mind, Elaine. I'll get the hors d'oeuvres. *(Exits)*

ELAINE: There's a nice plate of snacks in the refrigerator. I mean, I bet they're nice. Simone is so smart.

SYLVIA: Aren't you smart?

ELAINE: Oh, no. We used to be just alike in smartness—we both weren't. Then suddenly Simone was.

SYLVIA: After she and Gerald got married.

ELAINE: After she and Gerald got married.

SYLVIA: Why didn't you and Gerald get married?

ELAINE: I'm not sure...How'd you know about that? It wasn't...

SYLVIA: Serious between you.

ELAINE: Serious between us. It happened more than once, you know. Boys fell out of love with me when they met Dorothy, I mean Simone.

SYLVIA: Boys are two-faced.

ELAINE: Two-faced. And men...

SYLVIA: Are no better.

ELAINE: Let me tell you.

SYLVIA: It was awful.

ELAINE: It was awful. I'd get a date, I'd date a guy for a while, then he'd turn around...

SYLVIA: And invite Dorothy to the prom.

ELAINE: To the prom, yeah. A boy does stuff with me in the dark, but when the lights go on....

SYLVIA: And it's time to show somebody off—

ELAINE: He's with Dorothy.

SYLVIA: She changed her name.

ELAINE: I'm not suppose to talk about it.

SYLVIA: Gerald changed her name.

ELAINE: Oh, you *know*. Yeah. He thought it was more corporate. You don't work with Gerald, do you?

SYLVIA: No.

ELAINE: What do you do?

SYLVIA: I'm the psychic.

ELAINE: Don't tell Gerald. He doesn't believe in that kind of thing.

SYLVIA: He's starting to.

ELAINE: I've tried some psychic stuff. The one with the pencil. You stare at the pencil and try to make it move from here to here. It made me nuts. I finally picked up the pencil and moved it.

SYLVIA: It doesn't count unless they move by themselves.

ELAINE: I know.

SYLVIA: There's times when I want to pick them up and move them myself. But it doesn't count unless they do it on their own.

ELAINE: Or in groups. If you have, say, five pencils, then they have to do it on their own in a group by themselves—one of the women in my class is black.

SYLVIA: Really?

ELAINE: Uh huh. She says there's a lot of prejudice in dog competitions.

SYLVIA: I never would have thought of that.

ELAINE: Yes. She says there's hardly any black judges. No best-in-show judges are black—I wasn't always fat.

SYLVIA: It's harder when it comes on you later in life.

ELAINE: That's what I think. People don't like fat people.

SYLVIA: I do. I like people to look well fed.

ELAINE: Oh, I don't. I don't want to be seen with them. And sometimes, when a person is fat and says that they have, you know, like degrees and stuff, I don't believe they really have them. I think they're lying.

(Enter GERALD *and* GLADYS. GLADYS *carries the snacks.)*

GERALD: Here we go.

SYLVIA: *(To ELAINE)* Snack now. Don't eat after nine. *(To plate)* Oh, my, oh my goodness, just look at all that.

GLADYS: *(To SYLVIA)* Yes, pretty nice, huh?

GERALD: It looks good to me.

SYLVIA: What's that one?

GLADYS: Clam.

SYLVIA: Where's the mustard?

GLADYS: You don't put mustard on a clam.

SYLVIA: We didn't have clams anymore. Or mustard. *(Eating)* Oh, nice. *(She takes some clams and sits down.)*

GLADYS: Put them on a plate.

GERALD: Gladys...

SYLVIA: I'm sorry. I'm very excited about clams.

ELAINE: That's how *I* get. We never have nice stuff like this, so I overeat it when I see it. *(Eating)*

SYLVIA: *(Mouth full)* Eat now, don't snack after nine.

ELAINE: *(Mouth full)* I'm going to try it.

GLADYS: *(To ELAINE)* Those are very fattening.

GERALD: Gladys...

GLADYS: Just trying to help.

ELAINE: Why did Simone fix them? She knows I'm on a diet!

GLADYS: I fixed them.

GERALD: Simone made these.

GLADYS: I made them.

GERALD: Well, they look like the ones Simone always makes.

GLADYS: I *always* make them.

GERALD: Simone—

GLADYS: No. Me.

GERALD: ...Well, they're very nice.

GLADYS: Thank you.

(Doorbell)

ELAINE: I hope that's Bobby come back.

SYLVIA: *(goading her)* Simone's recipe?

GLADYS: *Mine*! I mean—...no, my recipe.

*(*GERALD *answers the door. It is* WAYNE *and his briefcase.)*

GERALD: Yes? Can I help you?

WAYNE: *(Points)* Gerald?

GERALD: Yes?

WAYNE: How do you do? I'm Wayne Holt.

ELAINE: Hi Wayne, I'm Elaine.

WAYNE: Hi, Elaine, I'm Wayne. ...uh...ha *(Nervous laugh)*

ELAINE: And that's Sylvia.

*(*GLADYS *hangs up his coat without comment.)*

WAYNE: *(To* GLADYS*)* Hello Simone. I'm sorry I'm late.

GLADYS: Simone is not here. *(Pointedly)* Okay?

WAYNE: *(To* GLADYS*)* What...

ELAINE: You're not late. Francis isn't here, either.

WAYNE: *(To* GLADYS*)* Simone, what's...?

GLADYS: *Simone is not here.*

*(*GLADYS *and* GERALD *stand on either side of* WAYNE.*)*

SYLVIA: *(To* GERALD*)* He isn't on the list.

WAYNE: List?

ELAINE: Would you like a snack, Wayne?

WAYNE: Snack? Nooo. *(To* GERALD*)* I brought your portfolio.

GERALD: My portfolio?

WAYNE: *(Holds up briefcase)* Your portfolio. Holt-Simmington Investments.

GERALD: That's my investment banker.

WAYNE: Me. Wayne Holt.

GERALD: Oh. Oh! Waaayne...

WAYNE: Holt, yes. Do you want to look at it?

GERALD: Um, no, no. Simone does that.

WAYNE: *(To* GLADYS*)* Simone?

GLADYS: Is not here.

*(*GLADYS *exits to kitchen.)*

SYLVIA: *(To* GERALD*)* I have the list right here. No "Wayne Holt."

GERALD: Just...put that list away. What would you like... Wayne?

WAYNE: What's everybody else having?

SYLVIA: Water.

GERALD: No, you don't have to...we have everything. I've got everything. Wild Turkey, Glenlivet, martinis all mixed. Boodles, very dry.

WAYNE: Water.

GERALD: Water. I hope we don't run out of it.

SYLVIA: So do I.

ELAINE: Nobody's drinking tonight.

SYLVIA: Francis will drink.

*(*GERALD *looks at* SYLVIA.*)*

SYLVIA: Just a hunch.

ELAINE: Yeah. Then maybe the party will loosen up.

WAYNE: *(Worried)* Party?

GERALD: Elaine...

ELAINE: Well, you do seem a little tense to me, Gerald.

SYLVIA: You shouldn't worry about Bobby and Simone, Gerald.

ELAINE: What?!

GERALD: I'm not worried.

ELAINE: What do you *mean* he shouldn't worry about Bobby and Simone?!

SYLVIA: I mean he shouldn't...worry. They'll be back.

ELAINE: Oh. You mean, he shouldn't worry that they got mugged or something?

SYLVIA: Uh huh.

WAYNE: *(Confused)* Where are...

GERALD: Simone and Bobby went out. Separately.

WAYNE: ...Simone went...?

GERALD: Out, out. They'll be back. It's a very safe neighborhood.

WAYNE: Um.. So...your wife is...?

GERALD: *Out*! She'll be *back*. It's very safe.

ELAINE: Now Gerald, nothing's really safe.

GERALD: Elaine. It is *safe*, safe. It is statistically the safest neighborhood in the city.

ELAINE: What about the shampoo bottle?

WAYNE: What was that?

ELAINE: A lady—in this neighborhood—walking down the street in the middle of the day was struck down dead by a shampoo bottle. It was just knocked off a window ledge. Fifteen stories. Kerplop. I hate that; I just hate it.

WAYNE: ...The arbitrariness of it?

ELAINE: That's it. I don't like the arbitrariness of it. If I have to go, I want to go because of *me*, not because of an elbow bonking a bottle. You know?

WAYNE: I do. I do know.

ELAINE: *(Happy)* You do?

*(*WAYNE *sneezes.)*

ELAINE: Bless you. You all right?

WAYNE: *(Through sneezes)* Yeah...It's just...Is there a cat?

GERALD: Of course not.

WAYNE: I think it's...*(Sniffing* SYLVIA*)* It's your perfume.

SYLVIA: Really? That's terrible. *(Happy)* I'll go shower!

WAYNE: If it's not too much trouble...

GERALD: What?

SYLVIA: *(Happy)* No trouble. No trouble at all!

ELAINE: There should be towels....

SYLVIA: I saw them. *(Exits)*

WAYNE: I just hate that.

ELAINE: Oh, I don't know.

WAYNE: I'm so out of control when I sneeze.

ELAINE: Yeah, but that's the good thing about a sneeze. That, and how it makes your skin *think*. It's kind of like an orgasm—I mean...oh, dear...oh, no...oooooooo—

WAYNE: *(Helping her out)* I never thought of it like that.

ELAINE: *(Miserable)* Yeah! Nobody ever thought of it like that.

WAYNE: But that's good.

ELAINE: Good?

WAYNE: Yes, very good.

ELAINE: *(Hopeful)* It is?

WAYNE: Yes, yes, it is. You made it up. It's like an original thought.

ELAINE: Like Bobby?

WAYNE: ...Who's Bobby?

GERALD: Wayne! Did you get a drink?

WAYNE: Yes, I did.

GERALD: So. You're my investment banker.

WAYNE: Yes, for some time now.

GERALD: I didn't know you were...I mean...I mean, I don't know what I mean. How about a martini?

WAYNE: My office is in the back. Simmington's the one you see if you peek through the windows. Simmington's bright, open, shall we say, white, face instills confidence in the minds of the investors. With a black face in the front, well, everybody always waits for the black quarterback to throw an interception. You know what I mean?

ELAINE: That's not true anymore. I saw it on Weekend Sports Roundup.

WAYNE: How's that?

ELAINE: It's not true anymore. They said. It used to be true; it isn't true anymore.

WAYNE: Oh. When did this happen?

ELAINE: December. January, maybe.

(Reenter SIMONE *and* BOBBY. GLADYS *enters, hangs coats.* WAYNE *and* GLADYS *exchange glances.)*

BOBBY: Look who I found.

SIMONE: Hi, hi everybody! We're back. Hi!

GLADYS: *(To* WAYNE*)* Please don't say anything.

WAYNE: Okay.

BOBBY: *(Referring to* SIMONE'*s fur)* Feed those furry little woodland creatures, Gladys.

ELAINE: Hi, Simone.

SIMONE: Elaine! Oh, you look so sweet in your outfit. *(They hug. To* WAYNE*)* Oh, hello. I'm Simone.

GERALD: Simone, silly. You know Wayne. Wayne Holt.

BOBBY: Hi. You work with Gerald?

WAYNE: *(He is amazed, but restrained.)* No.

SIMONE: Wayne...who?

GERALD: Holt, dear.

WAYNE: Holt-Simmington.

GLADYS: *(Pointedly)* Your investment banker.

SIMONE: *(Suddenly nervous)* Yes?

GERALD: He handles our money. You arranged it.

SIMONE: Well, of course, I know that. I need a drink. Does anyone else need a drink?

GERALD: Everybody.

WAYNE: Context.

GLADYS: *(To* WAYNE*)* Please...

SIMONE: What?!

WAYNE: Seeing me out of context. You didn't recognize me because I'm not in my office, behind my great big desk.

SIMONE: Where is Sylvia?

ELAINE: She's taking a shower.

BOBBY: *(To* WAYNE*)* I thought you worked with Gerald.

WAYNE: Why's that?

BOBBY: Because he's acting different.

ELAINE: It's subliminal body language. It's like dogs.

BOBBY: Elaine!

ELAINE: Dogs, all dogs, eat, drink, sleep, and go to the bathroom. But that's where the similarities end and the peculiarities begin.

BOBBY: What do you know about dogs?

ELAINE: I just mean, that if a person understood about dogs—then—that person, whoever she was, would also understand about people. The ways in which people behave, you can always tell who is who.

BOBBY: I can't.

(Enter SYLVIA. *Listens.)*

ELAINE: Well, that's true. Bobby doesn't bother to remember people.

BOBBY: Just famous people I don't bother.

ELAINE: He only knows the names of three actresses.

BOBBY: One brunette, one blonde, one redhead. Saves brain cells.

SYLVIA: White?

GLADYS: *(An outburst)* Of course white! Brunette is a white person with brown hair. Blonde is a white person with blonde hair. Redhead is a white person with red hair. These persons are always women.

GERALD: Gladys...

WAYNE: I know a black woman with blonde hair.

GLADYS: She can't be a "blonde."

WAYNE: She's going to be crushed.

BOBBY: All famous people become a few famous people. Saves brain cells.

WAYNE: Who are all famous black people?

BOBBY: All famous black people are two famous black people. Richard Roundtree.

WAYNE: Harry Belafonte—

BOBBY: Richard Roundtree is Harry Belafonte.

WAYNE: But Harry Belafonte came first.

BOBBY: Brain-cell conservation. Diana Ross.

WAYNE: Cecily Tyson?

BOBBY: Diana Ross *is* Cecily Tyson.

ELAINE: *(To* WAYNE*)* Does this offend you?

WAYNE: Oh, I won't know until after I've thought about it.

BOBBY: He's not offended. We're all brothers under the skin.

WAYNE: We aren't all brothers—but we are all connected.

BOBBY: How's that?

WAYNE: We are. We're all connected.

ELAINE: Is this Biblical?

WAYNE: In any city, a person is only three people away from knowing everybody in the city, every single person of the eight million people.

ELAINE: Why?

WAYNE: Well, here I am, right? And there's somebody all the way across town, right? Now, I don't know this man. But when you consider all the people I know, then all the people that the people I know, know; then all the people that the people I know, know, know—somebody knows this man across town. Three people.

BOBBY: I thought it was six.

WAYNE: Well, it's three.

ELAINE: We're connected?

WAYNE: Yes. I don't know you, but I'm connected to you through... *(Starts to point to* GLADYS, *then points to* GERALD*)* ...his wife. Whoever she is.

(A short silence)

ELAINE: Where did you find Simone, Bobby?

BOBBY: In the laundry room.

ELAINE: Was anybody else there?

BOBBY: It's nine o'clock.

ELAINE: Oh, I can't snack anymore.

BOBBY: What do you mean was anybody else there? What a silly question.

SIMONE: It's the laundry room. It's nine o'clock. All the maids have gone home.

ELAINE: Well, Gladys is still here.

WAYNE: Doesn't anybody in this building do his own laundry?

SIMONE: I don't know. Gladys, does anybody in this building do his own laundry?

GLADYS: There *is* a woman does her own laundry, but she dresses like a maid.

ELAINE: There wasn't anybody else in the laundry room?

BOBBY: No.

ELAINE: Well.

BOBBY: Well, what?!

ELAINE: Well, you were gone for a long time.

SIMONE: Stop it, Elaine.

BOBBY: Right. I threw Simone over one of the dryers and we had it on.

SYLVIA: One of the washers.

SIMONE: You're being silly, Elaine. Stop it.

GERALD: What do you mean, "one of the washers?"

WAYNE: *(To* ELAINE*)* Would you like to go...I mean...for a walk?

ELAINE: A walk?

BOBBY: How dare you?

WAYNE: How dare I what?

BOBBY: You invited my wife on a walk!

WAYNE: Wife?

GERALD: Over the washers, what? Over the, what?

SIMONE: Could you please finish your sentences? You're making me very tense.

WAYNE: *(To* ELAINE*)* I didn't know you were a wife.

GERALD: Maybe Bobby should take you back to the laundry room and calm you down.

SIMONE: I should have brought up the chips.

ELAINE: *(Erupting)* You certainly should have because you're so cute when you eat them.

WAYNE: I didn't know...

SIMONE: Does anybody need a drink?

GERALD: They're all drinking water.

SIMONE: That's ridiculous. *(Assertive)* I'll take care of this.

GLADYS: Would you like *me* to take care of it?

SIMONE: No, I do this. Bobby, vodka and soda. Twist of lime. Gerald, you'll need another. Okay. Proper glass, proper bottle, proper amount. Here. Wayne?

WAYNE: White wine cooler, please.

SIMONE: ...Really? Okay. Elaine, the usual?

ELAINE: *(To* SYLVIA*)* Can I drink after nine o'clock?

SYLVIA: Tonight you can because it's a party.

BOBBY: What about nine o'clock?

ELAINE: It's a surprise.

BOBBY: Where's our surprise? There's supposed to be a surprise, Gerald.

*(*GLADYS *looks in the records.)*

GERALD: Elaine is going on a diet.

BOBBY: Well, that's a surprise.

GERALD: We deliver. *(To* GLADYS*)* What are you doing in the music, Gladys?

ELAINE: I'll have one of those sweet green things that you make.

SIMONE: Coming right up.

ELAINE: Bobby never lets me get the drinks.

SIMONE: Sylvia?

SYLVIA: Martini, please.

GERALD: But, when I asked you—

(GLADYS puts on a record.)

SIMONE: Did Gladys bring out the goodies?

GLADYS: How else would they have gotten out?

ELAINE: Oh, that's nice. *(The music)*

(A salsa record plays. ELAINE swings along to it.)

GERALD: Is that a record? Let me see. *(Looks at cover)* This isn't ours. *(To SYLVIA)* Did you bring this?

SYLVIA: I didn't bring anything.

GERALD: This isn't one of our records.

ELAINE: I want to dance.

BOBBY: You are dancing.

ELAINE: I want to dance with a person.

BOBBY: Don't look at me.

WAYNE: Um...I'll dance with you, Elaine.

ELAINE: Okay.

BOBBY: Dance, Sylvia?

SYLVIA: Yes! Yes! Please!

ELAINE: Bobby, what are you doing?

BOBBY: What's it look like?

ELAINE: You never dance. *(To WAYNE)* He never dances.

SIMONE: Have another drink, Gerald.

SYLVIA: You *never* dance?

BOBBY: I occasionally never dance.

ELAINE: You dance so well.

WAYNE: Do I really?

ELAINE: Yes. Just bend your arm at the elbow.

WAYNE: Oh, I will. Thank you.

SIMONE: *(To GERALD)* You don't think *we* should dance, do you?

GERALD: Of course not. Give me that drink.

ELAINE: Actually, you should bend your knees sometimes, too.

WAYNE: Oh. Yeah, that feels better, you're right.

SYLVIA: *(To* BOBBY*)* You're a good dancer.

BOBBY: Thank you. So are you.

GERALD: Who brought that record?

GLADYS: I brought it. Years ago.

(Doorbell)

GERALD: Francis!

*(*GERALD *opens the door for* LOUISE *and* STANLEY. *Dancers dance;* STANLEY *enters doing a peculiar walk.)*

GERALD: What...?

LOUISE: Gerald? I'm Louise, that's my husband, Stanley, and that's his walk. Sorry we're late.

GERALD: What...?

SYLVIA: *(To* GERALD*)* Not on the list.

SIMONE: Hi. I'm Simone, that's Sylvia dancing with Bobby, and Wayne dancing with Elaine.

ELAINE: Hello, hello.

LOUISE: How do you do?

STANLEY: Hello.

*(*GLADYS *takes their coats.)*

LOUISE: *(To* GLADYS*)* Hi, how are you?

GLADYS: Dandy.

BOBBY: *(To* STANLEY*)* Is that dancing?

STANLEY: No. *(Proudly)* This is my ecological walk.

BOBBY: Nice.

STANLEY: Thanks. I developed it recently, and it's working.

BOBBY: What does it do?

STANLEY: Cuts down on methane emissions.

GERALD: *(Starts to pant)* What's happening? What's happening?

STANLEY: Well, you see, it's getting warmer. Methane combined with carbon dioxide heats up the atmosphere.

LOUISE: Stan's a climatologist.

(GERALD continues to pant. SYLVIA hears.)

SIMONE: What, Gerald, what?!

GERALD: We're outnummmmmmmberrrrred!

(GERALD pants; FRANCIS appears at the door.)

FRANCIS: Hello. I'm not too late?

SYLVIA: I'd say you were just in the nick of time.

(Blackout)

END OF ACT ONE

ACT TWO

Scene One

(The living room. GLADYS *looks around. Enter* SYLVIA*)*

SYLVIA: Interesting crowd.

GLADYS: It's time you were leaving.

SYLVIA: Where is everybody?

GLADYS: Back there. I have them safely separated.

SYLVIA: Why do they have to be separated?

GLADYS: You know why they have to be separated.

SYLVIA: No, I've never seen this part.

GLADYS: You haven't?

SYLVIA: This is all new.

GLADYS: *(Happy)* Oh. Well. They have to be separated because *because,* he's not ready.

SYLVIA: No?

GLADYS: No! He's not, he has to be ready, and he's not.

SYLVIA: Who's not?

GLADYS: He! Him! G—G—G—...

SYLVIA: You can do it.

GLADYS: G—G—

SYLVIA: Gerald?

GLADYS: Yes, that's the one.

SYLVIA: I'm not leaving yet. *(Beat)* He can't see me.

GLADYS: Who?

SYLVIA: Him.

*(*WAYNE *enters.* SYLVIA *makes herself invisible.)*

WAYNE: There you are.

GLADYS: Mr Holt! Having a good time?

WAYNE: Oh. Well. *(Surprised)* I'm actually having an *okay* time. But I'm very confused.

GLADYS: This will all become clear. I promise.

WAYNE: *(Brief pause)* All right. Just one thing. Have I done anything illegal, *Gladys*?!

GLADYS: ...Oh, no, nothing like that, no.

WAYNE: They *know* that you invest their money?

GLADYS: Simone knows. She begged me to do it. G—G—G-...

WAYNE: Gerald.

GLADYS: Thank you, doesn't know.

WAYNE: Interesting. What else do you do for the family?

GLADYS: You'd be surprised.

WAYNE: I don't get surprised. *(Beat)* I don't know what I'm supposed to do.

GLADYS: Socialize.

WAYNE: I don't socialize.

GLADYS: Yes. It's very good for business.

WAYNE: *(Wavering)* I've never believed that.

GLADYS: Yes, it's true. You should try it.

WAYNE: Is socializing ...talking to Elaine?

GLADYS: Yes, really, yes, you should.

WAYNE: I'll try it then. *(Exiting)*

GLADYS: Yes, give it a try. Socialize.

SYLVIA: That was very well done.

GLADYS: I don't need your approval, thank you.

(GLADYS exits. LOUISE enters with a sketch pad.)

SYLVIA: What've you got there?

LOUISE: *(Sees her)* Oh, hi. This is just a thing.

SYLVIA: That's good. It's me!

LOUISE: Thanks.

SYLVIA: Is this yellow part...water?

LOUISE: Yeah.

SYLVIA: You must be paying attention.

LOUISE: An artist has to pay attention.

SYLVIA: You're an artist—well, obviously you are.

LOUISE: I'm a designer. I did this place.

SYLVIA: Beautiful job. Splendid bathrooms.

LOUISE: *(Indignant)* I didn't do the bathrooms. I don't do big tubs. I almost didn't take the job.

SYLVIA: How did they convince you?

LOUISE: *They* didn't convince me, I never met *them*. I just met the uh— *(Points off)*.

SYLVIA: The uh—? *(Points)*

LOUISE: Yeah. Gladys. I came here, and the place was black, all black. There had been some big, I don't know, mistake, well clearly. And I met Gladys, and I thought she was the lady of the house.

SYLVIA: How's that?

LOUISE: Tea. She gave me tea. She apologized for the depressingly black room, knew exactly how she wanted it, you know, redone. She made all the decisions, picked out all the fabric. She poured us *tea*. Convinced me to take the job in spite of the big tubs.

SYLVIA: How did she do that?

LOUISE: She let me use Stan's experimental fabric. Looks real good, doesn't it?

SYLVIA: ...It does.

LOUISE: Silk whey.

SYLVIA: Silk...?

LOUISE: Whey. As in curds and. Just think of it as cheese cloth. It's all edible.

SYLVIA: How sensible.

LOUISE: Sure, for when you get tired of looking at it, or in some future emergency—

SYLVIA: It becomes lunch.

LOUISE: Lunch. I wanted to see how it was holding up. So when Gladys called...

SYLVIA: You came right over.

LOUISE: I came right over. With my sketch pad. I'm supposed to draw everybody.

SYLVIA: That's nice.

LOUISE: Yeah. For the game. Some game we're gonna play when everybody's ready. I'm going to go do the wife. She's very interesting looking.

SYLVIA: *(Happy)* Pink.

LOUISE: Well, they're all pink.

SYLVIA: Really?

LOUISE: Oh, yeah. Haven't you noticed that?

SYLVIA: I'm not an artist.

LOUISE: *(Complimented)* Oh. Well.

SYLVIA: What do you think of them?

LOUISE: I hardly know them.

SYLVIA: I mean *all* of them.

LOUISE: *(Whisper)* White people?

(SYLVIA nods. LOUISE sits.)

LOUISE: Sometimes I can meet a person and not notice right away that they're white.

SYLVIA: Really?

LOUISE: Yes. And sometimes, I can listen to a person on the radio without wondering if they're white.

SYLVIA: My.

LOUISE: Yes. I think that's real progress.

SYLVIA: How did it used to be?

LOUISE: Well, first off, when I'd meet some white person, I'd get like this hot flash of anger because of all the things I *knew* a white person wouldn't understand.

SYLVIA: What kind of things?

LOUISE: Oh, just getting-around kind-of-things, you know; me and Stanley will be making pained-animal noises at some lady in furs, and people look at us like we're nuts, just because we're black.

SYLVIA: *(Brief pause)* You don't think some *white* couple, some white couple that was making pained-animal noises at a lady in furs, you don't think they'd get looked at like they were nuts?

LOUISE: I didn't used to. Now, sure, now.

SYLVIA: You've been working on this?

LOUISE: Oh, yeah. Like crazy. See, Stanley is very worried about garbage. See, uh, I got to stand up to say this. *(She stands and walks* STANLEY*'s walk.)* "Hate creates violence, and violence creates garbage, and we don't have enough places to put garbage. We must avoid hate to avoid violence to avoid garbage." I'm going to go do the wife.

*(*LOUISE *exits.* WAYNE *enters with two glasses.)*

WAYNE: Hi!

SYLVIA: Hi.

WAYNE: I'm socializing. *(Holds up glasses)*

SYLVIA: How's it going?

WAYNE: Not too bad. *(Goes to bar)*

SYLVIA: Fix me a drink.

WAYNE: Fix *you* a drink?

SYLVIA: It's very social.

WAYNE: Martini coming up.

SYLVIA: You remembered.

WAYNE: I did, didn't I.

SYLVIA: Yes, that's quite social.

WAYNE: Yeah!

SYLVIA: You're a banker?

WAYNE: Investments. You?

SYLVIA: I'm the psychic.

WAYNE: What's your specialty?

SYLVIA: Making things move on their own.

WAYNE: Like you look at a pencil and it moves?

SYLVIA: Or you look at nine pencils and they move.

WAYNE: I always want to pick it up and move it. I've been looking for a psychic.

SYLVIA: For investment banking?

WAYNE: It's cheaper than real-time data access.

SYLVIA: Is this an offer?

WAYNE: I'd have to interview you.

SYLVIA: What's *this*?

WAYNE: *This is socializing. (Hands her a drink)*

SYLVIA: I can't take a job. I'm just passing through.

WAYNE: Oh.

SYLVIA: But we can still socialize.

WAYNE: *(He returns to bar, makes another drink while attempting banter, a deeper voice.)* What do you think of our little town?!

SYLVIA: I've barely seen it.

WAYNE: I'm sure you'll find it adequate.

SYLVIA: Maybe you could show me around.

WAYNE: *(Lost confidence, pain)* Oh, OH!...I don't go out.

SYLVIA: But you're here.

WAYNE: But I don't like it.

SYLVIA: What's the problem?

WAYNE: There's too many, far too many, too too many.

SYLVIA: Large numbers upset you?

WAYNE: Numbers? Numbers never upset me. Numbers orient me. Numbers—the larger the better—numbers—

SYLVIA: Large numbers *of people.*

WAYNE: Oh, well, yes, that upsets me.

SYLVIA: Why did you come?

WAYNE: I thought it was business. I don't get invited unless it's business.

SYLVIA: Why not?

WAYNE: I speak my mind.

SYLVIA: That can be a *good* trait, when it isn't a really *stupid* one. Ah, our host.

*(*GERALD *enters.* WAYNE *turns to talk to him, and* SYLVIA *makes herself invisible. She watches unseen. For different reasons,* WAYNE *and* GERALD *find this conversation extremely hard.)*

WAYNE: Hi! I'm socializing...Where did she go?

GERALD: No, please. Help yourself. *(Goes to bar)* I was just getting a refill myself. *(Pause)* So. How are the uh...stocks?

WAYNE: I brought your portfolio. Shall we—

GERALD: No, no, Simone does all that. I wanted to know how business was *in general.*

WAYNE: You were...socializing?

GERALD: Um...yes.

WAYNE: *(Socializing)* ...Business in general is good.

GERALD: *(Pause)* So, drink?

WAYNE: I have one. *(Holds it up)*

GERALD: Right. So. *(Pause)* Why do you drink that?

WAYNE: White wine cooler?

GERALD: Yes. It's such a...well, it isn't very...

WAYNE: I don't usually drink it. I'm only drinking it here.

GERALD: You don't have to. I have everything. You can have anything you want.

WAYNE: I can?

GERALD: Of course!

WAYNE: Maybe I'll have what I want later.

GERALD: ...Are we talking about a drink?

WAYNE: For now, I'll stick with this.

GERALD: ...Fine.

WAYNE: This drink comforts people. Other people. People who watch and listen to what I order to drink.

GERALD: Do many people listen to what you order?

WAYNE: I'd say so, yes.

GERALD: And these people need comfort?

WAYNE: I'd say so, yes. Naturally not all of them do. But some people are afraid of a solitary black man; some people are afraid of black men in groups; some people are afraid of white men in groups; some people are afraid of a solitary white man; and so on.

GERALD: It depends on who the people are, who they're afraid of.

WAYNE: I'd say so, yes.

GERALD: Does it work? The white wine cooler?

WAYNE: Yes. A white wine cooler instantly demystifies a man.

GERALD: Hm.

WAYNE: You should try it.

GERALD: Well, I...

WAYNE: Don't need it?

GERALD: I wasn't going to say that.

WAYNE: *(Looks at glass)* And women.

GERALD: *(Worried)* What about it?

WAYNE: Women are very comforted by a white wine cooler. And that, I'd say, is key.

GERALD: ...I'd say, so, yes, I'd say so.

WAYNE: The world is very scary for women. We shouldn't compound that by ordering exotic drinks.

GERALD: I'd...say...so.

WAYNE: I'd say so. Women express fears we can't begin to understand.

GERALD: ...Just tonight, Simone expressed a fear.

WAYNE: Which Simone is that?

GERALD: Simone. There's only one Simone. My wife.

WAYNE: A remarkable woman. What fear?

GERALD: Daylight. Confounded by daylight.

WAYNE: Exactly what I mean. Who would think it? Daylight. And it's always disappointing, to hear these fears.

GERALD: No, no, it doesn't have to be. I think of it as a...surprise. She provides weekly surprises and...disappointments. But that's life, right? You find out your wife is confounded by daylight? That's a disappointment, and...it's a surprise. But you don't have to be disappointed by it. That's a wife.

WAYNE: I'd like to have a wife.

GERALD: I certainly recommend a marriage like mine.

WAYNE: I just want one wife.

GERALD: Well of course one wife. Just like Simone.

WAYNE: I think I'd like to have a wife...like Elaine.

GERALD: Too late. Elaine is Bob's wife.

WAYNE: I know.

GERALD: Elaine wouldn't be a good wife for you. She's not the executive-wife type.

WAYNE: You know Elaine well?

GERALD: Oh. Sister-in-law and all that, and, well, Elaine...and I, well we have history. Before Simone and I. Elaine and I broke up.

WAYNE: Can't take a fat girl to parties?

GERALD: Well, you *can*—why do you keep saying that?

WAYNE: Pardon?

GERALD: Oh, not you. Never mind. It really wasn't anything. Just one of those things. I mean, I liked her, but....

WAYNE: She was fat.

GERALD: Yes, no! I mean, that wasn't it. Elaine and I, well, I knew the type of woman I wanted to marry....

WAYNE: Thin.

GERALD: Elaine is not that fat. She's...

WAYNE: A sticky libidinous rub.

GERALD: It wasn't like that!

WAYNE: But that's how you wanted it.

GERALD: Why do you say that?

WAYNE: That's how *I'd* want it. Some people, through no fault of their own, inspire intense sexual feelings.

GERALD: ...That's what I think.

WAYNE: And it's always kind of a surprise, who it is who inspires it.

GERALD: Yes, I think you're right, yes.

WAYNE: It isn't logical, and it's occasionally disconcerting.

GERALD: Yes, yes!

WAYNE: What are you supposed to do when you walk into a stranger's house and find yourself attracted to the wife of another stranger?

GERALD: ...I am uncomfortable with this conversation.

WAYNE: That happens to me a lot.

GERALD: You get uncomfortable with the conversation?

WAYNE: No, the other guy does.

GERALD: ...I just want to say, that it wasn't a sweaty rub, Elaine and I, I mean. It was one of those things. And then I met Simone.

WAYNE: And everything became clear.

GERALD: Yes. You see the finances!

WAYNE: ...Quite.

GERALD: She helps me. I'd be lost without her little reminders. Little notes in the morning beside my cup. I refer to them during the day. Little notes.

WAYNE: I'm sure.

GERALD: There are things about a spouse that only a spouse knows. Simone is a different person in the dark. It's remarkable.

WAYNE: ...I'm sure it is...quite remarkable. And there's always the kids.

GERALD: No kids.

WAYNE: You *have* kids.

GERALD: No, we don't.

WAYNE: ...You don't?

GERALD: No, we don't!

WAYNE: What about the college fund?

GERALD: What college fund?

WAYNE: The college fund. Your, uh, Mrs, you... It was started years ago. For when the kiddies are ready for college.

GERALD: *(A complete loss)* Oh. Well. That's for the day...when the kiddies that we *will* have—some day—are ready for college.

WAYNE: It's a pretty tidy sum. That you have in the college fund.

GERALD: Well, that's com...fortating, I mean, con...sultating to know.

WAYNE: Elaine and Bobby have kids?

GERALD: No, thank goodness.

WAYNE: Yes. Mothers are very unavailable.

GERALD: ...That is *not* what I meant. I said "thank goodness" because with Bobby there would be no college fund, because with Bobby there is occasionally no rent fund.

WAYNE: Is that appealing to Elaine? I mean, does she like money?

GERALD: I don't...know if she...likes money. I mean, I suppose she...likes money most people like money except, of course, Bobby, who eschews anything remotely connected to the establishment—like money, and I don't have an appeal for Elaine because I don't *want* to have an appeal for Elaine and there is *nothing* between us, and we don't want anything between us, okay?

WAYNE: Yes, that's fine. ...Well, I think this has been very social.

GERALD: ...Social, yes.

WAYNE: Do you mind if I...? *(Picks up glass at bar)* I was getting a drink for—

GERALD: What, oh, yes, please, please join the party.

*(*WAYNE *exits with his two glasses.* GERALD *drinks and breathes.* SYLVIA *watches. Enter* BOBBY *and* FRANCIS.*)*

BOBBY: I'm sorry I asked, okay?

FRANCIS: And the one you wrote before *that* one, Bobby, I had to read with a dictionary by my side.

BOBBY: All right, Francis.

FRANCIS: And *I'm* literate.

BOBBY: Okay, already. *(To* GERALD*)* You're all flushed. You look like you're going to pop.

FRANCIS: *(To* GERALD*)* Do you need C P R, Gerald?

GERALD: Francis, Francis, what is going on?

FRANCIS: Strangers are drinking whiskey throughout your apartment.

GERALD: What are they doing here?

BOBBY: You invited them.

FRANCIS: Bobby thinks you invited them. Enlighten Bobby.

BOBBY: Maybe Simone invited them.

GERALD: They weren't on the list.

BOBBY: Did you invite Sylvia?

GERALD: Yes, I did. I did do that.

BOBBY: Maybe she invited them. Ask her.

GERALD: I don't want to seem stupid.

BOBBY: Aw, go on, Gerald. Step into the unknown.

GERALD: Maybe it's something that they do, and I don't know about it. Some social custom.

BOBBY: What "they?"

GERALD: They! Black people, you pretentious liberal ass!

FRANCIS: Go on, Gerald, ask her how she dared to invite all these black people into your home.

GERALD: It isn't that she invited black people, it's that she invited anybody.

FRANCIS: Really? I often arrive with four or five guests and you never even peep.

BOBBY: Gerald is afraid to peep at you, Francis. Gerald wouldn't want to contradict the divine emissary of hip.

FRANCIS: No, I think it's that my entourage has a different hue.

BOBBY: You may think it's an entourage; I think it's a school of piranha.

FRANCIS: They aren't piranha, Bobby. They are normal meat eaters who can't resist mammals lower down the food chain.

(WAYNE with his two glasses and STANLEY enter.)

WAYNE: *(To STANLEY)* I don't know how they fill it; I don't live here.

STANLEY: *(To FRANCIS)* It isn't a food chain; it's a food web.

FRANCIS: I was speaking metaphorically.

STANLEY: Yeah, they changed it a few years ago. Used to be food chain, now it's food web. Personally, I think food *grid* would be even more appropriate.

GERALD: Were you listening, Mr um?

STANLEY: Stanley. Yes, I was looking at the bathrooms. Who lives here?

GERALD: I, I do. And Simone.

STANLEY: No kids?

GERALD: No! I mean, no.

STANLEY: How *do* you fill it?

WAYNE: He's talking about the bathtub.

GERALD: We turn on the tap.

STANLEY: Four feet by eight feet by three feet. That's a big. Big. Tub. I'm a climatologist.

GERALD: Big?

STANLEY: We're losing our water.

FRANCIS: Not possible.

SYLVIA: *(Invisible)* Possible and likely.

FRANCIS: Water can neither be created nor destroyed.

GERALD: Who said that?

(STANLEY scrutinizes the edible furniture fabric while he speaks.)

STANLEY: That's *matter.* I'm not talking about matter. I'm talking about *water.* Water is not the same as matter. Water is water. And we're losing it.

FRANCIS: How careless.

GERALD: *(Looking under things)* Who said "possible and likely?"

STANLEY: It *is* possible and likely. From big tubs. And termites, of course.

FRANCIS: Termites? Where?

STANLEY: Everywhere; well, not here, but everywhere else. Tons of them. They eat wood.

FRANCIS: That's bad.

STANLEY: That's not the bad *part*. They produce methane.

FRANCIS: Is *that* the bad part?

STANLEY: Yes. The ice caps will melt, drought, famine, death. People should wash in bowls.

FRANCIS: Isn't there some danger of neglect when washing in a bowl?

STANLEY: Never. Where neglect occurs is in the bathtub.

FRANCIS: I assure you, I neglect nothing in the bathtub.

STANLEY: Everybody says that. I'll bet you, on occasion, just sit there, soak, read a book, maybe, then get out, thinking, "I must be clean, I've been sitting in the bathtub."

FRANCIS: No, I don't sit, I don't soak, I don't read. I wash. Quite thoroughly.

WAYNE: I just take a shower.

STANLEY: Talk about neglect. The shower.

BOBBY: And waste.

WAYNE: A short shower.

BOBBY: We should conserve.

STANLEY: Exactly. Exactly. I'm so glad to hear you say that. *(He hands out cotton swabs.)* Here. Here. Take one and pass the rest along.

WAYNE: What—?

STANLEY: Instead of a tub. A swab. Conservation.

WAYNE: This isn't going to get me clean.

STANLEY: It's for the little places. You?

FRANCIS: Not if it were the law, and I was in the privacy of my own home.

STANLEY: First, the ear.

WAYNE: No, wait, no. It says right on the box, do not stick in ears.

BOBBY: Ouch! I poked myself.

STANLEY: This goes better if people help each other out. That's what Louise and I do.

FRANCIS: You and Louise *know* each other.

STANLEY: We *know* each other because we help each other out. Bring your swab over here, Bobby.

WAYNE: ...I feel peculiar about this.

FRANCIS: The understatement of the decade.

BOBBY: Come on, guys. It's conservation.

FRANCIS: *(To* BOBBY*)* No, no, no. Never let some party other than yourself look at an area of yourself that you yourself haven't thoroughly examined.

GERALD: *(To* WAYNE*)* Did you hear somebody say "possible and likely" before?

WAYNE: No. I'm here by mistake.

GERALD: Mistake? What mistake?

WAYNE: I'm not supposed to be here.

GERALD: *(Thinking a major explanation is at hand)* Speak, Man, speak! What mistake?!

WAYNE: *(Holds up glasses, explains)* I'm supposed to deliver this drink. I'm socializing.

GERALD: *(Disappointed)* Oh.

WAYNE: *(To* STANLEY*)* I didn't use this yet. Do you want it back?

STANLEY: Visual aids.

WAYNE: Sure. Sure. Bye, bye. *(Exits)*

STANLEY: Some people need visual aids. Bowls. I'll be right back. *(To* GERALD*)* Oh. This room? *Very* nice.

GERALD: ...Thank you.

STANLEY: *(Big smile)* Silk whey. Me.

*(*STANLEY *exits.* FRANCIS *goes to the bar.* SYLVIA *remains invisible.)*

FRANCIS: I mean, really. Drink, anybody?

GERALD: *(Panting)* Yeah, yeah.

BOBBY: He's right, you know. The water? I read something.

*(*LOUISE *enters with her sketch pad.)*

LOUISE: Is this the Boys' Club or can anybody join.

FRANCIS: If Bobby can join, anybody can join.

*(*LOUISE *sketches* FRANCIS.*)*

FRANCIS: What's this? *(The sketching)*

LOUISE: This is art.

FRANCIS: And I thought Bobby was the only artist at the party.

*(*BOBBY *goes to the bar.)*

LOUISE: You draw?

BOBBY: No. Write. Cheers.

LOUISE: Don't tell Stan you write.

*(*GERALD *extends his swab to* LOUISE.*)*

LOUISE: What's that swab doing in here?

GERALD: *(Trying to get to the bottom of things)* Did you and uh *Stan* have any problems finding the place?

LOUISE: Of course not.

GERALD: Sylvia's directions were...okay?

LOUISE: ...Whose directions? *(Suspicious, takes swab)* What has Stanley done?

*(*SYLVIA *makes herself visible.)*

GERALD: *(Startled, points)* Ahhhhhh.

BOBBY: Hi.

FRANCIS: Hello.

GERALD: *(To* BOBBY*)* Did you see that?

SYLVIA: *(Looking at the sketch)* Oh, you're doing Francis.

BOBBY: Let go of my arm, Gerald.

LOUISE: *(To* FRANCIS*)* What do you do?

FRANCIS: For a living?

LOUISE: Yes. I want to draw you in action.

BOBBY: Just draw him with a knife in his hand.

FRANCIS: And do Bobby with one in his back.

LOUISE: You a cook?

FRANCIS: I'm a literary agent.

SYLVIA: What kind of literature?

FRANCIS: Books, movies, magazines.

BOBBY: Television "literature."

FRANCIS: By all means, television literature. Television literature reaches people, Bobby.

BOBBY: Do you do portraits for a living, Louise?

LOUISE: I'm a designer. I did this place.

GERALD: What?!

LOUISE: Except those bathrooms. Somebody else did those.

GERALD: Oh. Oh! You must know *Simone*. And Simone knows *Wayne*. And you're married to *Stanley* and Sylvia was *invited*. Great, great!

SYLVIA: *(To* GERALD*)* But they weren't on the list.

GERALD: But it's a start!

SYLVIA: *(To* LOUISE*)* How's it coming?

LOUISE: Francis is done. I'll do our host, now.

GERALD: What are these for, anyway?

LOUISE: These are for the game.

GERALD: No. No game. Perhaps you should all go.

FRANCIS: Go?! You're sending me away?

GERALD: Yes, maybe this wasn't a good idea. I need to....

FRANCIS: I'm not going away until something fun happens.

GERALD: Fun?

FRANCIS: The big fun thing that makes the departure from my apartment worthwhile.

GERALD: The big fun thing?

FRANCIS: Yes, the big fun thing.

GERALD: But, ...I'm exhausted.

FRANCIS: Well, Gerry, you're going to have to rest up.

GERALD: *(Into it)* Rest up? *(Sits)*

FRANCIS: Sure, Gerald, rest up. *(At the bar)* I'll be host. Can I fix anybody a drink?

SYLVIA: We've been helping ourselves.

FRANCIS: Don't spare yourselves. Simone and Gerald have heaps. We can all take home a bottle. Right, Gerald?

LOUISE: I'm not walking out with stuff.

FRANCIS: Think of it as a party favor. *(Hands* LOUISE *a bottle)*

BOBBY: Gerald will call the cops.

LOUISE: *(Returns bottle to bar)* I'm not taking this. I'm putting this back, see? Did everybody see? I don't want somebody coming looking for this. I had a past life.

SYLVIA: *(Interested)* Where?

LOUISE: I got killed by Nazis.

BOBBY: Why do you think so?

LOUISE: Because what scares me worse than anything is white men in boots. Wintertime's real bad for me.

BOBBY: I'm afraid when the phone rings at night.

LOUISE: The doorbell's worse.

BOBBY: I'm afraid it's gonna be the cops. I'm gonna be accused of stealing.

LOUISE: You steal?

BOBBY: No.

LOUISE: Me neither, but I'm really afraid of being accused of it.

BOBBY: The drug store? at the exit? the buzzer?

LOUISE: That's the worst.

BOBBY: I imagine the buzzer goes off, and the security guard roughs me up and looks in my shopping bag, and there's something that fell inside, something I don't even notice. They say "Ah, ha!" and I'm dragged off. I stand in front of the judge and I can't even speak.

LOUISE: I know this fear.

BOBBY: It paralyzes you.

LOUISE: I know.

BOBBY: A person can't act. He can't.

LOUISE: She may want to.

BOBBY: He may want to. He may want to be part of the human chain around the Pentagon....

LOUISE: She may want to squirt mustard on mink coats.

BOBBY: But he doesn't.

LOUISE: Neither does she.

BOBBY: Because he can't risk it.

LOUISE: No way.

FRANCIS: The...Jail...Cell.

BOBBY/LOUISE. *(Together in horror)* Jail?

FRANCIS: The holding tank. Fifty people together in one cell. Shoulder to shoulder. Vomit, urine, sweat; men speaking in tongues, psychological and physical terror rising in your throat, suddenly you're surrounded by...

BOBBY/LOUISE. *(Exiting)* Ahhhhhh.

FRANCIS: Where are you two going?

BOBBY: Gotta find my girl.

LOUISE: I gotta find Stan.

(They exit. GERALD *stands. He is unsteady.)*

FRANCIS: Yes, Gerald? Need a drink? I'll get it. *(Goes to bar)*

*(*SYLVIA *stands in front of* GERALD *and makes herself disappear and reappear.)*

FRANCIS: Here you go. Open your hand, I insert the glass, now close your fingers.

GERALD: *(To* FRANCIS*)* Do you have...a piece of paper?

FRANCIS: Paper? Noooo.

GERALD: I have to find...I'll be right back. That was...

(He starts to exit, returns, touches SYLVIA *gingerly on shoulder.)*

GERALD: I'll be right back. *(Exits)*

FRANCIS: May I do that?

SYLVIA: Sure.

FRANCIS: *(Touches her shoulder)* Gerald doesn't think you're real. ...I scared Bobby.

SYLVIA: And Louise.

FRANCIS: They should get over it. Fears are incapcitating.

SYLVIA: What are *you* afraid of?

FRANCIS: Power ties, the wrong hair cut, superconductors. I have to rein in my imaginings, or I don't sleep nights.

SYLVIA: What does a literary agent do?

FRANCIS: A literary agent makes people meet each other.

SYLVIA: That's what I do.

FRANCIS: If you put the right people in a room together, the right things will happen. Amazing things.

SYLVIA: Yes, Yes!

FRANCIS: It's an important skill.

SYLVIA: I know.

FRANCIS: Then I get out of the way so they can work it out.

SYLVIA: *(Disappointed)* Don't you...help out?

FRANCIS: No, some agents do that. That helping business. I call people up. Have them meet.

SYLVIA: So, you're never actually there.

FRANCIS: No. I'm never *there*. I'm at home. In my apartment slash office. By the phone. I like it. It's very—

SYLVIA: Safe.

FRANCIS: Yes. I confess, I like safety.

SYLVIA: Why don't you do something for Bobby?

FRANCIS: Bobby Bobby Bobby. Bobby, I'm afraid, does not write for the majority.

SYLVIA: *(Sincerely)* And you can tell because you're a white man and that's the majority?

FRANCIS: ...I'm a what?

SYLVIA: A white man. *(Explaining)* I wondered if you could tell about Bobby writing for the majority because you're a white man?

FRANCIS: *(Amazed)* A white man. I'm a white man.

SYLVIA: What are you—

FRANCIS: *(Laughing)* A white man. I'm a white man.

SYLVIA: But you must know that.

FRANCIS: No, no, as it turns out, no. I just thought I was a man.

SYLVIA: What's wrong with Bobby's writing?

FRANCIS: From my point of view, from my white male point of view—

SYLVIA: You should get over this.

FRANCIS: I'll try. Bobby's Writing. By the time you get to the verb, you can't remember the subject. Every sentence.

SYLVIA: It's bad?

FRANCIS: It's multi-syllable words and multi-punctuation mark sentences. I can't sell it. What do *you* do?

SYLVIA: Currently I'm trying to save things. For the future.

FRANCIS: What are you saving tonight?

SYLVIA: The clam. Among other things.

FRANCIS: Please save the clam. Do you know when we're getting our surprise? When Gladys called, she said there was going to be a surprise.

SYLVIA: I've heard mention of a game.

FRANCIS: Well, I'm getting a little tired of waiting for it. *(Pause)* I don't suppose you'd like to leave with me?

SYLVIA: You shouldn't leave. Something...amazing might happen if you stay in this room.

FRANCIS: Something amazing might happen if we leave.

SYLVIA: I really can't leave.

FRANCIS: I understand. I'm sure it's nothing personal.

SYLVIA: Oh, no, it is personal. It's entirely personal.

FRANCIS: Does this have something to do with whiteness?

SYLVIA: Not at all. You see, it doesn't matter to you whether I go with you or not.

FRANCIS: Well... That's true.

SYLVIA: I know. And for me to go with you, why, it would have to be life or death.

FRANCIS: Life or death? That would be a surprise.

SYLVIA: Or at least matter.

BOBBY: *(Enters)* I can't find anybody, I can't find anybody.

FRANCIS: Prison, jail cell, men speaking in tongues—

(Enter SIMONE.*)*

BOBBY: Stop it! Simone, I've been looking all over for you.

(BOBBY *hugs* SIMONE *desperately.)*

SIMONE: Bobby! Bobby! What's wrong with you?

BOBBY: He said prison.

SIMONE: Where's Gerald?

BOBBY: The hell with Gerald; I'm scared.

(Enter STANLEY *and* LOUISE.*)*

STANLEY: You don't have to get rid of the tub.

SIMONE: The tub?

STANLEY: No, it's perfect. A compost bin slash worm box. Install an infrared light so you can watch the happy little worms at work eating your garbage.

SIMONE: I beg your pardon?

STANLEY: You can wash at the sink. With your swab. The worms won't mind.

SIMONE: ...Would you like a drink?

LOUISE: Stan, you're leaving out steps.

STANLEY: Conservation is complicated.

SIMONE: *(Relief at understanding)* Oh! Conser*vaaaa*tion!

STANLEY: And the silk whey is a great first step.

SIMONE: ...Thank you.

STANLEY: The longest journey begins with the first etcetera. Now you need to pick out a place for paper—newspaper, junk mail, cardboard—the dining room I think. A corner of the dining room. Paper all wrapped up with string, kept in a corner of the dining room, collected once a week and taken to the paper place; you'll find one. Okay, paper's under control. What next? Organic waste, composted in the bathtub, with the help of the worms. Compost harvested weekly and collected on Saturdays. Taken out to the curb by the youngest child who waits on the corner for the compost truck to arrive. Friendly compost-truck driver empties the compost into the truck. Truck takes the compost to the country and distributes it among the farmers. Happy farmers come for their free compost. Organic, no pesticide vegetables grown in naturally composted soil. A healthy nation, a healthy world.

(Brief pause)

FRANCIS: What if you don't have a child?

STANLEY: What?

FRANCIS: A youngest child to wait on the curb for the happy compost truck driver?

BOBBY: Francis, you're making me mad.

STANLEY: Uh...

FRANCIS: That's why these idyllic plans fall apart, Stan. Little hitches develop.

BOBBY: I mean, we'd hate to inconvenience you just to save the planet, Francis.

FRANCIS: You've set yourself up for a big disappointment, Stanley.

SIMONE: I don't think it's too much to ask of a person. I could collect newspapers and compost.

FRANCIS: You're not ready to share your bathtub with worms, Simone. Nor do you have a kid to wait at the curb for the friendly compost truck driver. And there *is no* friendly compost truck, and if there were a friendly compost truck driver, he'd dump it into the nearest river after dark.

STANLEY: We have to start, we have to start.

BOBBY: What are you doing to get the word out on this, Stanley?

STANLEY: That's not my job.

FRANCIS: *(Goading* STANLEY*)* Write it up, Stan. We can make it a book.

STANLEY: A book? You make books?

LOUISE: Oh, dear.

FRANCIS: I get them published.

STANLEY: Ahhhhhh.

FRANCIS: I don't burn them. I don't make *heat*. I'm not evaporating *water*. I'm merely trying to publish a book or two.

STANLEY: And what are books made of? Paper. And what is paper, but *trees*.

FRANCIS: I thought the problem was water.

STANLEY: Trees *are* water.

LOUISE: Stanley. You're losing your logic.

STANLEY: Most books are garbage.

BOBBY: That's for sure.

FRANCIS: Bobby writes books.

BOBBY: Hey! Hey! They don't get published. I'm cool.

STANLEY: Books are the worst.

*(*GERALD *enters. He has taken off his outer shirt and is wearing a sheet around his shoulders.)*

LOUISE: No, Stan. Remember? Books are the *fourth* worst.

GERALD: I am trying to rest up. But the noise is impossible.

STANLEY: Well, you're right. Packaging is the worst, and fossil fuels, and coal, and elephant-foot umbrella stands, and burning down the rain forest....

BOBBY: *(Happy)* Packaging! You mean packaging...like advertising?

STANLEY: Yes, yes. Advertising. Packaging. Very destructive.

BOBBY: *(Points to* GERALD*)* Him. Advertising.

STANLEY: *(Disbelief)* Nooo.

GERALD: I've almost figured it out, but you're all going to have to be quiet.

STANLEY: Oh, no. Can't you see, isn't there some way you could.... *(Losing it)* Shrink-wrapping really makes me mad. Styrofoam meat trays—double seals, bubble packs. Why, why?!

FRANCIS: Because nothing sells unless it's in a package, Stanley.

STANLEY: You're killing the planet.

GERALD: Okay! We'll deal with the planet later, in the meantime—

(Enter WAYNE *and* ELAINE. ELAINE *is wearing one of* SIMONE'*s furs. It is very tight.)*

ELAINE: I want this coat!

STANLEY: Oh, misery, furs!

BOBBY: Take that off! Elaine, that's animals! Take that off!

WAYNE: It looks real good.

*(*LOUISE *and* STANLEY *whimper.)*

SIMONE: You can have it. Don't get upset.

BOBBY: Take it off, take it off, Elaine.

ELAINE: I'm sick of you! I want this coat!

BOBBY: Seals! Baby seals! Remember the zoo?!

ELAINE: Mine! It's mine.

BOBBY: This is a politically irresponsible coat! Take it off! Take it off!

*(*BOBBY *takes coat from* ELAINE. *She is in her slip.* LOUISE *and* STANLEY *stop whimpering.)*

ELAINE: Give that back.

BOBBY: Wearing baby seals is globally irresponsible.

ELAINE: You don't believe that. You're having a speaking frenzy, give it back!

BOBBY: ...Speaking frenzy? I gotta write that down. *(To* ELAINE*)* You have a pencil?

ELAINE: I'm naked.

BOBBY: Baby seals, Elaine.

*(*WAYNE *takes sheet from* GERALD *and puts it around* ELAINE.*)*

WAYNE: Pardon me. Here. Put this on.

BOBBY: What are you doing? *(Rips off sheet)* You put a sheet on my wife. What are you thinking of?!

WAYNE: I thought I'd cover her up.

BOBBY: With a sheet?! A sheet?! White people in sheets? Have you lost your whole mind?

WAYNE: *(Points to* GERALD*)* He was in a sheet.

BOBBY: I'm not married to him.

LOUISE: *(To* STANLEY*)* How do you think the wearing sheets compares to the wearing seals?

STANLEY: There's no comparison at all.

BOBBY: There certainly isn't.

STANLEY: Give her back the sheet.

BOBBY: No. Give her back the seals.

STANLEY: No, the sheet.

BOBBY: No, the...huh.

(They all look at the sheet and coat. GLADYS *enters and takes* GERALD*'s hand.)*

GLADYS: Come along.

GERALD: They took my sheet.

GLADYS: Come along.

*(*GLADYS *and* GERALD *exit. The others gather around the sheet and coat.)*

SYLVIA: Amazing.

Scene Two

(The living room, the women. The sheet is gone. ELAINE *is dressed.)*

ELAINE: *(To* SIMONE*)* I was showing Wayne the apartment. I was showing off *your* apartment. We entered the bedroom, I opened the closet—

GLADYS: You shouldn't show off what's not yours.

ELAINE: Give me the coat, Simone.

*(*ELAINE *puts on coat;* LOUISE *whimpers.)*

ELAINE: There were all these rows and rows of expensive beautiful things. I knew I couldn't fit into any of the dresses. I had to take off all my clothes to make the coat go around me. *(To* LOUISE*)* Would you please stop that, this is not a puppy.

LOUISE: I'm sorry; it's a reflex.

GLADYS: You're only interested in those clothes because they're Simone's.

ELAINE: I'm interested in those clothes because my clothes are garbage, garbage!

GLADYS: You have dog training. You don't need clothes, too.

ELAINE: Mind your own business.

GLADYS: Just trying to help.

ELAINE: Bobby's not going to let me wear this coat, anyway.

SIMONE: I'll talk to him.

ELAINE: No thank you!

LOUISE: Stan's ideals get harder on me every year.

ELAINE: Right. If somebody gives you a coat, a coat that's already made out of already dead seals, I don't see what difference it makes.

LOUISE: Stan can clear that up for you.

ELAINE: Great! Somebody else "clearing it up for me." Everybody thinks I'm stupid because I'm fat.

SIMONE: You're not fat.

GLADYS: She's fat.

SIMONE: What?

LOUISE: Not really fat—

GLADYS: A porker.

SIMONE: Oh. Elaine, I'm sorry. I didn't know you were fat. What can I do?

ELAINE: Of course I'm fat. That's why I'm not rich. I need something to eat. *(Starts to exit)*

GLADYS: Don't go in there.

*(*ELAINE *exits to kitchen.)*

SIMONE: *(Goes to bar)* Does anybody need a refill?

GLADYS: I'll get the drinks. *(Goes to the bar)*

SIMONE: I do the drinks.

GLADYS: I'll do it.

SIMONE: But, I know what everybody's drinking.

GLADYS: I'll take care of it.

SIMONE: *(Desperate)* No, I'm going to do it. I have to do it!

GLADYS: Okay, Simone. You get the drinks. One last time. *(Exits)*

SIMONE: *(To* SYLVIA*)* Would you like me to fix you another drink?

SYLVIA: No thank you.

SIMONE: *(Disappointed)* Oh. Louise?

LOUISE: No thanks.

SIMONE: *(Fixes herself a drink)* I don't think Elaine is fat.

SYLVIA: You want to look like that?

SIMONE: Oh, no, of course not.

*(*ELAINE *enters. She looks as if she has seen a ghost.)*

SIMONE: Did you find something to eat, Honey?

ELAINE: Uh...

*(*STANLEY *enters wearing only a towel.)*

STANLEY: I'm sorry.

LOUISE: Oh, no. *(Head in hands)*

STANLEY: I was giving a demonstration. I'm really sorry.

LOUISE: Stanley, please put on your clothes.

STANLEY: Uh, right. *(Exits)*

ELAINE: He was washing. Uh...they were all...

LOUISE: Stan thinks that we should wash in a bowl.

SIMONE: A *bowl*? What kind of *bowl*?

LOUISE: A bowl, bowl.

SIMONE: A big bowl? A bowl you stand in?

LOUISE: A *bowl*. You put some water in a bowl, use a cloth, and wash yourself.

SIMONE: Oh, a *bowl*.

LOUISE: Yes, a bowl.

ELAINE: Well, I think that was a very good...description. Couldn't he just...describe it to people?

LOUISE: Stan thinks people need visual aids.

(Enter the men, GERALD, BOBBY, WAYNE, STANLEY *are pulling on their clothes.)*

BOBBY: *(To* STANLEY*)* A story, full of adventure. We can make it an adventure story, an environmental adventure story. Robin Hood plugs the ozone hole.

STANLEY: No books, Robert.

FRANCIS: It wouldn't sell, anyway, *Bobby.*

BOBBY: *(To* FRANCIS*)* It might sell. The environment's hot.

WAYNE: It's true. Investors are asking about corporate environmental policies.

FRANCIS: Yes, and pigs are asking about wings.

SIMONE: Gerald, did you actually wash?

GERALD: It seemed...very social.

WAYNE: Yeah.

STANLEY: Gerald was best.

GERALD: I was?

BOBBY: He didn't wash his hair.

WAYNE: *(To* BOBBY*)* Hair washing was not required.

BOBBY: I always wash my hair.

STANLEY: Brush it more, it won't need washing.

BOBBY: We can put that in the novel.

STANLEY: Sorry, Robert. Books are part of the problem.

SYLVIA: *(To* FRANCIS*)* You aren't wet.

FRANCIS: I didn't wash. I mean, really.

GERALD: *(Looking around)* Where is...everybody?

SIMONE: Everybody is here, Gerald.

FRANCIS: *(Sarcastic)* How about a video, Stanley. You and Bobby and Wayne and Gerald here. *HOW TO WASH.*

ELAINE: A how-to? Bobby could write the instructions.

BOBBY: Elaine!

FRANCIS: Right, Bobby could write the instructions. The four of you could star. Sell it to T V.

STANLEY: T V promotes packaging. Packaging is garbage.

FRANCIS: Gerald, are you going to let him insult your profession like that?

GERALD: Everybody isn't here.

BOBBY: Stan, how about...a *little* book. A little *manual. Hundreds of little lists, what each person can do—what each person can eat.* To reduce his, or her, methane emissions. Little lists of recipes.

STANLEY: *(Interested)* Little lists?

BOBBY: On recycled unbleached paper. With perforated edges, to be torn out and displayed on the refrigerator.

STANLEY: *(He's into it)* Perforated edges?

*(*GLADYS *reenters wearing an extradordinary outfit and flat shoes.)*

GERALD: There you are.

STANLEY: You look very nice.

GLADYS: Thank you.

SYLVIA: Nice shoes.

GLADYS: Thanks!

STANLEY: Is there a mop?

GLADYS: You don't mop. You're a guest.

STANLEY: Well, in there. *(Points to kitchen)* A spill.

GERALD: I'll mop!

*(*SIMONE *gasps.)*

GLADYS: *(Crossing to* GERALD*)* Are you sure you want to mop.

GERALD: I'm sure. Um. Where is the mop?

GLADYS: In the broom closet.

GERALD: Broom closet?

GLADYS: *(Gently)* The tall skinny door in the kitchen.

GERALD: Thank you. *(Looks at her again)* And a...piece of paper?

GLADYS: By the phone.

GERALD: Thank you. Thank you. *(Exits)*

SIMONE: *(To* GLADYS*)* Would you like me to fix you a drink?

GLADYS: I'm sorry, Simone, but you've fixed your last drink.

*(*LOUISE *pets* ELAINE'*s coat.)*

ELAINE: They're dead! They're *already* dead.

STANLEY: But still so beautiful.

ELAINE: Of course, they're beatutiful. That's the point.

STANLEY: Human skin is no match for it.

ELAINE: My skin...?

STANLEY: No comparison.

WAYNE: Now, wait a minute.

ELAINE: I want to go home.

BOBBY: I'm not leaving. We're right on the brink.

WAYNE: *(To* STANLEY*)* Now look what you've done.

ELAINE: *(Looks at her wrist)* My watch.

SIMONE: What about your watch?

ELAINE: It's gone.

LOUISE: Oh, swell.

STANLEY: Louise...

LOUISE: Let's get out of here.

BOBBY: Wait, why?

STANLEY: Let me get my shoes.

SIMONE: What's happening?

LOUISE: Let's go.

FRANCIS: You can't go. There's a missing watch.

ELAINE: They didn't steal my watch.

LOUISE: This can't be happening.

BOBBY: Louise, we've gotta put this in perspective.

STANLEY: Where are my shoes?

BOBBY: Stanley, we're on to something; you can't go now.

ELAINE: Sometimes I take it off when I wash.

STANLEY: I took them off when we washed. *(He exits.)*

WAYNE: *(To* ELAINE*)* Where did you wash?

ELAINE: I didn't.

WAYNE: Oh.

*(*LOUISE *dumps her purse on the floor.)*

SIMONE: Oh my.

LOUISE: There!

ELAINE: Where?!

LOUISE: You see? I don't have it.

ELAINE: Oh...I thought when you said "there"—

LOUISE: I said "there" because "there!" it isn't there.

STANLEY: *(Enters)* Does anybody have a—What—? Oh, I have to borrow this. *(Takes pen from* LOUISE'*s dumped purse and exits)*

LOUISE: Stan—

STANLEY: I'll be right back. There's some writing emergency in there.

*(*ELAINE *stares at* LOUISE'*s arm.)*

LOUISE: Stanley, I want to go—

FRANCIS: It'll look bad if you go.

LOUISE: *(To* ELAINE*)* What are you staring at?

ELAINE: Nothing.

LOUISE: You were. You were staring at my arm.

ELAINE: Nice arm.

LOUISE: At the watch on my arm.

ELAINE: No no.

LOUISE: *(Holds her wrist out)* This...is...mine.

*(*ELAINE *covers up* LOUISE'*s watch.)*

ELAINE: Of course it's yours.

LOUISE: *(Confused)* ...Maybe it isn't mine.

ELAINE: It is, it is.

LOUISE: *(Worried)* ...Maybe I have a whole secret life. A life of which I am totally unaware.

BOBBY: Elaine let go of Louise's arm.

STANLEY: *(Entering with shoes)* Yes, please let go of Louise's arm.

ELAINE: I'm sorry.

GLADYS: Did you check your pocket?

ELAINE: My...?

GLADYS: Pocket.

ELAINE: Oh, wow. Look. I took it off to try on Simone's coat. You can't wear a Timex with a fur. Thanks, Gladys.

LOUISE: Let me see. *(Looks at watches)* My goodness.

ELAINE: They're the same.

LOUISE: *(To everyone)* I'm terribly sorry.

BOBBY: Don't be silly, Louise. Paranoia is the only way to go. Paranoia isn't even paranoid anymore.

WAYNE: I agree with that, Bob. Paranoia is good sense. Whenever I hear about a crime on the news, I think, please let him be white, don't let him be black, and if he isn't white, and he is black, you know what I do, Bob? I buy a new suit. Brooks Brothers. Expensive. Shine my shoes. Get my hair cut. I do not allow that anyone will mistake me for the black who is a criminal.

BOBBY: I do that, Wayne. When I'm in Europe, in some bar, and somebody is making a fuss, I think "oh, please don't let him be an American. Let him be German." And then when he isn't German and he is American, I become ultra polite, courteous to a fault, so people don't think that all Americans are louts.

ELAINE: I know how you feel. Whenever I'm in a car and somebody runs over something, I think, "oh, please don't let it have been some live thing."

(Pause. Everyone looks at ELAINE.*)*

BOBBY: You don't drive.

ELAINE: Oh, I know. And that makes it worse. How can you turn to somebody who's driving you around and say, "I hope that wasn't some live thing you just hit."

BOBBY: Elaine, Honey, that's not at all what we're talking about.

WAYNE: Of course it is! This coat was once some live thing that somebody hit!

*(*ELAINE *and* WAYNE *share a revelation. They pet the coat.* GERALD *enters.)*

GERALD: I wrote. And I mopped! And I washed. With this little pen. I figured it out. It's an idea. And now I'd like to tell you my idea. The one I wrote down. I want to say. It's all become clear. You see, when you are disturbed by a situation, maybe the thing that is making you disturbed is the *real thing* that's going on, and the thing that you *want to be happening* is just the dream. *(Pause,* GLADYS *stands next to him, he looks at her.)* And maybe some things that you *have* noticed, and you said to yourself "I don't notice that," maybe you *did* notice them all along, but if something *had not happened*, you'd just keep thinking that you *had not noticed. (Brief pause)* And the list just proves it!

GLADYS: I think it's time to play the game.

SYLVIA: Ah yes, the game.

ELAINE: Yes, please.

LOUISE: The game?

STANLEY: You said you wanted to go.

LOUISE: I drew all the pictures, Stan.

STANLEY: Bring on the game.

FRANCIS: Is this going to be as much fun as "who stole the watch?"

SYLVIA: *(To* FRANCIS*)* Are you going to join in?

FRANCIS: No, somebody has to keep track of when each one of you loses his or her mind.

WAYNE: You didn't wash, and now you won't play? Come on.

LOUISE: Here, Gladys. *(*LOUISE *gives* GLADYS *the sketches)*

STANLEY: What's the game?

GLADYS: A person, Simone, for example. Looks at a drawing. The rest of you look at her face to figure out who she's looking at.

SYLVIA: A psychic game!

GLADYS: Yes. Go ahead, Simone.

SIMONE: Okay. *(She looks at a sketch.)*

BOBBY: Gerald. That's Gerald.

FRANCIS: No, Gerald wouldn't inspire that look.

SYLVIA: So you are playing.

FRANCIS: That was commentary, not participation.

ELAINE: She's looking at dogs.

WAYNE: I think she's looking at you, Elaine.

SIMONE: Uh...

STANLEY: I don't know who it is.

LOUISE: I agree with Wayne.

ELAINE: Who is it? Tell us.

SIMONE: Uh...Elaine.

LOUISE: We were right, Wayne.

STANLEY: *(Passes it around)* Oh, this is very good, Louise.

LOUISE: Yeah, thanks.

ELAINE: Let me see me. *(Looks at it)*

WAYNE: One point for me, one point for Louise.

ELAINE: Look at all those doggies. You drew me with all these doggies.

WAYNE: They look like my dogs.

ELAINE: *(Impressed)* Three labs. Three great big labs.

STANLEY: That's a lot of methane.

SIMONE: Let's play some more! Who am I looking at, now?

WAYNE: You know, Simone should get points. For psychic sending. Right?

SIMONE: Two points for me.

WAYNE: I'll keep track of the points.

LOUISE: Stan, you feeling okay?

STANLEY: I feel...uneasy...like somebody...

ELAINE: Like somebody is looking at you?!

STANLEY: Yes. Just like that.

FRANCIS: I guess Stanley! I get a point.

BOBBY: No, you don't.

FRANCIS: Is it Stanley, Simone?

*(*SIMONE *nods.)*

ELAINE: We're all psychic.

SYLVIA: You're all paying attention.

FRANCIS: I get a point. What's the score, Wayne?

BOBBY: You're not even playing.

WAYNE: Francis gets a point.

BOBBY: That's not fair. That is not fair.

FRANCIS: Yes, Bobby? Are you losing the game?

BOBBY: It's Stanley's point, not yours.

SIMONE: *(To change the subject)* Who am I looking at now?

ELAINE: My turn! Who am I looking at? *(She looks at* WAYNE *and giggles.)*

FRANCIS: *(Calmly raises hand)* I guess Wayne. I get another point.

BOBBY: No! You're not playing and you don't get points.

SYLVIA: Maybe Francis *needs* points.

FRANCIS: No, I don't. I don't need points.

SYLVIA: Is it Wayne, Elaine?

ELAINE: Yes it is. This is great.

GLADYS: It's your turn.

GERALD: My turn?

GLADYS: Yes, I think it's time.

*(*GLADYS *hands* GERALD *a sketch. He looks and smiles.)*

BOBBY: Simone.

FRANCIS: Definitely Simone.

ELAINE: Simone.

SYLVIA: Anybody else?

STANLEY: I'll go with Simone.

LOUISE: Me, too. Simone.

WAYNE: I'll go along. Simone.

SIMONE: Yeah, it's me, all right. *(Pause)* Gerald? Is it me?

GERALD: Hmm?

SIMONE: The sketch. It's me, isn't it?

GERALD: Yes! Yes, it is. Excuse me, I have to find...

SIMONE: Where are you going? Show us the sketch.

FRANCIS: Yes, Gerald, show us the sketch.

GERALD: There's this little piece of paper. I need to find it.

FRANCIS: Show us the sketch.

GERALD: *(Hugs sketch)* Sure, sure, just as soon as I find that little piece of paper...

SIMONE: Give us the sketch, Gerald.

GERALD: I will, I will, I just need a minute....

(FRANCIS snatches sketch.)

GERALD: Oh, no.

SIMONE: That's not me.

FRANCIS: No, that's not a bit like you.

SIMONE: Gerald, is this a joke?

GERALD: *(Searching pockets)* I just need that little piece of paper—

BOBBY: *(Looking)* Isn't that Gladys?

WAYNE: I'd say so.

ELAINE: Looks like Gladys to me.

GERALD: This will all become clear...here! *(Finds a piece of paper in his pocket)* Here it is. Oh, no. It got wet when I mopped. It got all wet.

GLADYS: Let me see. *(GERALD's piece of paper)*

WAYNE: Nobody gets any points.

GERALD: All the ink's run together. My idea.

GLADYS: Well, look, you can still make out a few words. What's that?

GERALD: Real thing.

GLADYS: Right. And those?

GERALD: *(Happy)* Be happening.

GLADYS: And down there?

GERALD: Notice. Notice.

SIMONE: *(Beat)* Oh, no.

GLADYS: Oh, yes. Real thing be happening. Now. *(Points at things in apartment)* This, this, that, those. I did it all, and I'd say it was all mine.

GERALD: ...Notice?

GLADYS: Little notes, next to your coffee cup. Me. A risk-free portfolio? My investment ideas. Mine.

GERALD: Real thing...

WAYNE: Yes, it's true, Gerald. Gladys and me, we're old friends.

ELAINE: So that's how Dorothy got smart.

GLADYS: The carpets, the wallpaper, the furniture, the designs.

GERALD: Um.

GLADYS: Me.

LOUISE: It's true, Gerald. She's the one.

GLADYS: The laundry, the cleaning, the shirts—not too stiff, not too soft, the social calendar, the cheese!

GERALD: Real thing...

GLADYS: Kisses on my neck. Reminders in the night. *Me* in the night.

SIMONE: Oh, dear.

GLADYS: It was me, every time.

STANLEY: Is this part of the game?

LOUISE: I think this is the real thing.

GLADYS: Simone, I'm sorry, but this arrangement isn't working out.

SIMONE: You're right. Gerald, this arrangement isn't working out.

GERALD: *(Reading)* Be happening.

SIMONE: This marriage isn't working. You're a faithless husband, and I hate that.

GERALD: *(Reading)* Notice. Notice.

SIMONE: Well, you are, even if you didn't notice. It's Gladys. In the dark. Gladys does everything. I don't get to do *anything* anymore. I'm dissolving, Gerald. I'm melting into the sheets. I want to learn a skill.

GLADYS: A job will be good for you, Simone.

SIMONE: Thank you, Gladys. I think so, too. I'm going to need one if I'm going to take care of Bobby.

ELAINE: No...

SIMONE: Yes. Elaine, I'm taking Bobby. It's been me and Bobby for a long time.

GERALD: Over the dryers.

SYLVIA: Over the washers.

BOBBY: Elaine...

ELAINE: Shut up, Bobby.

SIMONE: Sorry.

ELAINE: I know. It's not you. It's men. They can't help themselves once they see you. They feel that they have to have you, or die. It's always going to be that way.

WAYNE: *(Quietly, to* ELAINE*)* Pardon me, may I say something?

ELAINE: Oh, why not?

WAYNE: I don't find her attractive.

ELAINE: Oh, come on!

WAYNE: No, really. I don't find her attractive. Whereas, I think you're a real dish.

ELAINE: Dish?

BOBBY: Elaine, can Simone stay at our place?

ELAINE: Sure, but it's going to be the three of us for a while.

WAYNE: Well, no. It doesn't have to be.

ELAINE: You mean...?

GLADYS: Wayne has dogs, Elaine.

WAYNE: Three labs. It's a little tough to tell them apart....

ELAINE: Not for me, it isn't.

GLADYS: *(To* GERALD*)* We have to pick out a room for our daughters.

GERALD: Daughters?... Kids...?

WAYNE: The college fund.

SIMONE: The co-op board is going to flip.

ELAINE: Bobby always said "No pets."

WAYNE: My dogs are no problem. I let them go in the yard.

STANLEY: I hope you're picking up the droppings.

BOBBY: The droppings! Stanley, our book.

LOUISE: You could explain Silk Whey, Stan. *(She takes a bite out of a piece of furniture.)* The edible fabric of the future. Ummm.

STANLEY: Little lists?

BOBBY: Yes! Little lists, in a little, little book.

STANLEY: Perforated edges.

BOBBY: To tear out and post as little reminders.

SYLVIA: It's very reasonable.

ELAINE: Stanley, I want to learn how to walk your walk.

BOBBY: Me too, me too.

STANLEY: Walk?! My walk? My ecological walk? Great, great! Like this.

ELAINE: *(Behind him)* Like this?

WAYNE: *(Behind* ELAINE*)* Hey, that's it. You're doing it, Elaine.

BOBBY: Is this right? *(Gets in line behind* WAYNE*)*

LOUISE: That's it, Bobby. You're doing it. *(Gets in line)*

SIMONE: Me, too. *(Gets in line)*

GERALD: *(Sort of happy)* Kids? Daughters?

GLADYS: You better get in line, Gerald. *(He does, beat)* I said it. I said it! *(Gently)* Gerald, I said your name.

GERALD: Is that my name?

GLADYS: Gerald.

GERALD: It's beautiful.

*(*FRANCIS *goes to the closet for his coat.)*

FRANCIS: I'll get my own coat, Gladys.

SYLVIA: *(To* FRANCIS*, worried)* You're leaving?

FRANCIS: I think so.

SYLVIA: Oh, no. Don't you want to learn to walk, Francis?

FRANCIS: No.

SYLVIA: What about the little little book?

FRANCIS: It's been done. I mean, really.

SYLVIA: But they need you.

FRANCIS: Looks like they're doing just fine to me. *(Exits)*

ELAINE: Simone, I'm not taking that coat.

BOBBY: Elaine, that's great; that is so great!

ELAINE: *(To* BOBBY*)* What do you care?!

SIMONE: I'm not taking it either.

GLADYS: *(To* SYLVIA*)* I'm not going back.

SYLVIA: I know.

GLADYS: And I don't think you should stay.

SYLVIA: Say it again.

GLADYS: Gerald! Gerald!

GERALD: I'm walking, I'm walking, Gladys.

SYLVIA: Okay. I have another errand, anyway.

GERALD: Gladys, are you going to walk?

GLADYS: Yes, here I come. *(Gets in line in front of* GERALD*)*

GERALD: Gladys, you're not going to leave, are you? I mean, I washed and mopped, and I'm walking now. And maybe I can, I don't know, do something else.

GLADYS: That's good, Gerald. That's very good.

*(*LOUISE *puts the fur coat on the floor. They walk around it.)*

LOUISE: Okay, everybody, try the sound. *(Whimpers, they all whimper.)*

SYLVIA: Bye. Bye bye.

GLADYS: *(Walking)* Do it like I do it, Gerald. Watch me.

(Lights fade on party. SYLVIA *walks to a table on a cloud.* FRANCIS *is already sitting there, watching T V.)*

SYLVIA: What are you watching?

FRANCIS: Some science fiction movie.

SYLVIA: Yes, I know that one. The one that ends abruptly.

FRANCIS: Yes, the end was quite abrupt. Some excessively bold woman running around in muck. Still, I'd like to see a more satisfying ending.

SYLVIA: So would I.

FRANCIS: What now?

(SYLVIA picks up menu.)

FRANCIS: I read it.

SYLVIA: Then it must be time for... *(Snaps at T V)*

FRANCIS: *(Horror)* That was...

SYLVIA: Your life. Want to watch it again? *(Snaps)* Let's watch it again. *(Snaps)* Say, why don't we watch it again.

FRANCIS: No, not again. *(Breath)*

SYLVIA: No, let's watch it again. *(Snaps)*

FRANCIS: No. Ah, ee, oh, ah. *(Breath)*

SYLVIA: I think we should watch that again. *(Snaps)*

FRANCIS: Ah, ee, oh, ah.

SYLVIA: Yeah. *(Snaps)*

FRANCIS: Ah, ee, oh, ah.

(FRANCIS watches in horror. Lights begin to fade to black.)

END OF PLAY

THE SNOWFLAKE AVALANCHE

No snowflake in an avalanche ever feels responsible.
Stanislaw Jerzy Lec

for Mark, the accordion bandit

THE SNOWFLAKE AVALANCHE premiered at The Group Theatre in Seattle Washington in January 1993. The cast and creative contributors were:

RUSSELL	Anthony Lee
TIM	Marcus Rollins
POLLY	Demene Hall
JANET	Olga Sanchez
THOMAS	Lawrence Ballard
SANDY	Christine Salvador
Director	Mark Lutwak
Set design	Robert Dahlstrom
Costumes	Frances Kenny
Lights	Darren McCroom
Music/sound	Wayne Horvitz
Props	Steven Wiehs
Stage manager	Robin Macgregor

CHARACTERS & SETTING

RUSSELL, *an attorney*
TIM, RUSSELL*'s son, ten*
POLLY, *a translator.* RUSSELL*'s wife,* TIM*'s mother*
JANET, *a former activist*
THOMAS, *a fisherman.* JANET*'s husband*
SANDY, *a spirit who dances. Played by a girl or young woman. It could be a puppet.*

RUSSELL, TIM, *and* POLLY *are African Americans;* THOMAS *and* JANET *are Native American Indians.*

Places: A house, a prison, a municipal building, a coastline.

Note: The action of the play is continuous between scenes; no blackouts except at the end of the acts. Happily, none of these characters smoke or end statements with up inflections.

ACT ONE

Scene One

(A living room in a house on a lot in a town in a country on a continent in the world. RUSSELL *is alone, then* TIM *enters with a painting. He places the painting on an easel in front of* RUSSELL.*)*

TIM: There. I finished it. It took a long time. Really long. I started it *yesterday.*

RUSSELL: *(Trying to be supportive)* My, yesterday.

TIM: Yeah. And I worked on it *all day* after school. And then today, I came home and worked on it *all day* until now.

RUSSELL: A two-day project.

TIM: Yeah, a *long* time, because, you know, you said maybe I didn't spend enough time on them. I spent a lotta time on this.

RUSSELL: Well, time's not the only part.

TIM: Dad. Dad. I know time's not the only part, but you *said* I didn't spend enough time on them. You *said* I should take more time. I spent a lot of time on this.

(Brief pause)

RUSSELL: I don't know what you want me to say, Tim.

TIM: Well, Dad, you should say *something.* It took two days.

RUSSELL: ...I'm glad you're devoting more time to your paintings.

*(*TIM *takes the painting from the easel.* POLLY *enters.)*

POLLY: I'm taking the car...look at all that blue! Tim, that's great.

TIM: *(Tearing painting)* Two days! *(Exits)*

POLLY: Don't tear it...Timmy—What? What did I do?

RUSSELL: You shouldn't say things you don't mean.

POLLY: I meant it.

RUSSELL: Polly, you tell him it's great and the rest of the world ignores it. What's he supposed to think then?

POLLY: What did you say to him?

RUSSELL: Nothing bad. *(Playfully)* Nothing to destroy the budding artist lurking within his frail bones.

POLLY: ...He's just a little boy.

RUSSELL: So we should lie to him because he's a little boy?

POLLY: It wasn't a lie.

RUSSELL: There are people standing in line out there, all waiting to lie to him. We shouldn't lie to him.

POLLY: Russell. It wasn't a lie.

RUSSELL: Okay, Polly. It was a *great* picture. Now he'll paint a better one. *(Brief pause)* Where are you going?

POLLY: To the library. Did you need the car?

RUSSELL: *(For the tenth time)* We're the only family on Long Island with one car.

POLLY: The old man across the street has one car.

RUSSELL: Yeah, but he doesn't drive.

POLLY: We don't need two cars.

RUSSELL: If you want the car and I want the car we need two cars.

POLLY: That doesn't happen.

RUSSELL: It's happening now.

POLLY: No it isn't, I can go to the library tomorrow. ...Russell, take the car. Take it.

RUSSELL: ...I was going to visit Thomas.

POLLY: Oh. Janet already left.

RUSSELL: Left where? Where did she go?

POLLY: To visit Thomas. She took the baby.

RUSSELL: Why didn't she wait for me?

POLLY: She didn't know you were going.

RUSSELL: Why didn't she ask me? Oh, great. Now I've got to worry about her, too. What did she say? What did she say exactly.

POLLY: *Exactly,* I don't remember. She took extra diapers, she thought she'd be gone all day.

RUSSELL: What is she going to do, hitchhike? Oh, great, great!

POLLY: Well, I guess we could issue an all-points bulletin.

RUSSELL: I'm just worried, Polly.

POLLY: Russell, she went with you yesterday. She can figure it out.

Scene Two

(A jail. RUSSELL *and* THOMAS. *A newspaper)*

THOMAS: How did my wife get to New York?

RUSSELL: She flew.

THOMAS: Janet flying. That's funny.

RUSSELL: Doesn't she like flying?

THOMAS: I was gonna ask, I forgot; talking on that telephone with the window between us made me stupid. ...Did it cost a lot, the airplane?

RUSSELL: Yeah.

THOMAS: Who paid?

RUSSELL: There's a fund, a defense fund. Money's coming in from all over the world. People want you to get off.

THOMAS: I wouldn't let me off.

RUSSELL: It doesn't help if you talk like that. Who brought you the paper?

THOMAS: It's from a program; everybody gets a newspaper. So we stay current.

RUSSELL: I haven't seen a paper in weeks.

THOMAS: Then you aren't as current as me. ...I want to see my daughter.

RUSSELL: You saw her yesterday.

THOMAS: From behind a window.

RUSSELL: It's not possible.

THOMAS: They let me see you.

RUSSELL: I convinced them I could handle you.

THOMAS: They think I'm going to hurt my baby?

RUSSELL: They don't want to risk it.

THOMAS: Seeing Janet and the baby, but not touching them, it's not real. In my cell, I can touch all the walls at once. It's not human.

RUSSELL: What did you expect?

THOMAS: I didn't expect.

RUSSELL: Thomas. I need you to tell me what happened.

THOMAS: I told you.

RUSSELL: I need you to tell me again.

THOMAS: Let me hold my daughter, and I'll tell you again.

Scene Three

(Another part of jail. RUSSELL, JANET, *holding baby)*

JANET: *(Explains)* I walked from your house to the train, took a train to Pennsylvania Station, got a subway, got a bus, crossed a bridge, here I am.

RUSSELL: Maybe I should try that.

JANET: It cost seventeen dollars, and you have to walk a lot, but, I think it's faster than the car.

RUSSELL: Are you going in?

JANET: Thomas got too sad yesterday.

RUSSELL: You're not going to visit him?

JANET: No, it makes him sad.

RUSSELL: You took a train and a subway and a bus and you're not going in?

JANET: Yeah, I'm not.

RUSSELL: ...Can I take you home?

JANET: We want to be near for a while.

RUSSELL: Well, I'll wait until you're done...being near, and then I'll take you back.

JANET: I got a round trip.

RUSSELL: You can use the ticket some other time. *(Brief pause)* Did you like flying?

JANET: No. It's very terrible. Thomas wouldn't like it.

RUSSELL: Why?

JANET: The first thing they say is what to do if the plane crashes. That's a terrible thing to say to a person right off. My father wouldn't fly. He could walk steel beams fifty stories up, but he wouldn't get in an airplane. He told me an old Indian proverb: Birds fly, human beings drive cars. I must take after my Indian side—I found it very terrible. Over the Rockies the plane bounced. The passengers became very quiet. The pilot said we were experiencing turbulence. We were experiencing terror.

RUSSELL: It *sounds* very terrible.

JANET: Yes, it was very terrible. At one point the plane dropped, it just *dropped*. The pilot came on the loud speaker and said he was buying us a round of drinks. There was a lot of laughing then.

RUSSELL: At least you got a drink.

JANET: I don't drink, Russell, what are you thinking of?

RUSSELL: Um, I'm sorry, uh...

JANET: Oh! Oh, no, sorry, *I'm* sorry. You don't know—drinking, it's not something that we do casually. We either "drink" or we "don't drink." And if we "don't drink" we tend to be kind of fussy about it. Of course, if we *do* drink we tend to be kind of fussy about that, too. Me and Thomas, we don't.

RUSSELL: Well, I won't forget.

JANET: *(Laughs)* Yeah, I guess you won't.

RUSSELL: You should tell Thomas about the flying.

JANET: I saw the spill. You can still see it from high up. Black beaches.

RUSSELL: ...How's the baby?

JANET: She's quiet. She doesn't cry, but she also doesn't laugh. Do you want to hold her?

RUSSELL: I...

JANET: Take her; she's sick of just me.

*(*JANET *puts the baby into* RUSSELL*'s arms.* RUSSELL *awkwardly holds her.)*

Scene Four

(The house. TIM *talks to* SANDY.*)*

TIM: They always come into my room, check up on me, make sure I'm in bed.

SANDY: They do this every night?

TIM: Every single night.

SANDY: Every night at the same time?

TIM: Yeah, before they go to sleep. They check on me.

SANDY: Wait until *after* they check on you.

TIM: After they check on me?

SANDY: Wait in bed, keep your eyes shut. When you hear the door close, open your eyes again. They'll think you're asleep, plus you'll be able to see in the dark.

TIM: I can see in the blackest dark.

SANDY: Me too.

TIM: The floor creaks here, loud.

SANDY: Step over it; walk silently; climb. Climb from ground to tree limb, to tree top, swing to vent cover! Yank vent cover from wall! Quietly. Slip into the vents.

TIM: The vents are really dirty.

SANDY: Get a towel so you don't spot up the walls.

TIM: It feels good in the vents.

SANDY: The heartbeat of the house is in the vents.

TIM: And it's really dark. It *feels* dark. I wish I could paint in the dark.

SANDY: Yeah, paint the special night messages!

TIM: But there's no way.

SANDY: Hold onto the messages until it's light.

TIM: They're too big.

SANDY: Keep them in your mind, you can do it.

POLLY: *(Off)* Tim?

(SANDY disappears. POLLY enters.)

POLLY: Who you talking to?

TIM: Just, you know, talking.

POLLY: ...Were you painting?

TIM: No. I was talking.

POLLY: Okay. Don't forget to wash before dinner.

TIM: I won't.

(POLLY exits.)

TIM: *(Quietly, at the vent)* Sandy? Sandy? Aw.

Scene Five

(The house. POLLY, JANET, *baby in a cradle, cleaning products, bucket, mop.)*

POLLY: *(For the tenth time)* Janet, you don't have to do this.

JANET: No, it's a good idea. It'll give me something to do. I won't feel like a...what's the word for somebody who just takes?

POLLY: You don't do that—

JANET: What's the word, anyway?

POLLY: I don't know, uh, suppliant?

JANET: I don't think that's the one I'm thinking of.

POLLY: You're not taking anything away from anybody.

JANET: You give me a room, you give me your cradle, you ride me around in the car.

POLLY: It's an *extra* room, nobody is *using* the cradle, and I take you in the car when I'm going *anyway.*

JANET: What you do for me isn't small, it's big. There's money, you know. The defense fund. We could stay in a motel on Eleventh Avenue.

POLLY: That doesn't mean you have to clean up after us.

JANET: I *want* to do this. I have *nothing* to do. My mind drifts when I read, I don't like T V, you're at the U N, Russell's at the court, Tim's in school, there's nobody to talk to, any kind of job somebody gives me, they're not going to let me keep the baby; this way I'll get to know you better through your mess.

POLLY: Okay, okay. Do you want this? *(A cleaning product)*

JANET: Nah, I just use hot water, so when I'm done, I can dump it down the drain.

POLLY: What else would you do with it?

*(*POLLY *exits with bucket and mop.* JANET *looks toward the sink.)*

Scene Six

(The house, TIM, *baby, cradle,* SANDY*)*

TIM: Look, Sandy. She's really little. Look at her hands. They're really little.

SANDY: Everybody starts out like that.

TIM: Not Dad.

SANDY: Yes, Dad, too.

TIM: That hand is pretty small.

SANDY: See if she'll take your finger.

TIM: Look! She's holding my finger.

SANDY: She's smiling. She likes you.

TIM: I think she likes me, too.

SANDY: Say something to her.

TIM: I don't know what to say.

SANDY: It won't matter; she can't understand you.

TIM: Okay. *(Thinks it up)* Don't worry about how little you are; it's normal. She's smiling bigger!

SANDY: Your information was a big relief.

TIM: Look at her kick.

SANDY: Her feet are hot.

TIM: What should I do?

SANDY: Take her socks off.

*(*TIM *takes socks off baby.)*

TIM: Yeah! Now she's *really* smiling. I hope her face doesn't crack. I'm going to have a baby like this one, *teach* her stuff.

SANDY: Yes. Show her things.

TIM: Take her climbing in the vents. Adventures. I'll teach her how to swim.

SANDY: You don't know how to swim.

TIM: I'll learn and then I'll teach her.

JANET: *(Off)* Tim?

*(*SANDY *disappears.* JANET *knocks and enters.)*

JANET: *(Looks around, she heard talking)* Hello. How's the baby?

TIM: Her socks came off.

JANET: That happens. She's sleeping?

TIM: No, she's just quiet.

JANET: I'm glad you like to watch her.

TIM: It's easy.

JANET: She's a good baby. She misses her father.

TIM: How come he's in jail?

JANET: Didn't your parents tell you?

TIM: No, but they probably just forgot.

JANET: He killed someone. Someone bad.

TIM: Oh man, oh man. They don't want me to know that.

JANET: Are you sorry I told you?

TIM: Yeah, I am. I don't want to know that.

JANET: Don't worry. Your father is helping.

TIM: Yeah, but killing somebody, I don't know if Dad can *do* anything about that.

JANET: He'll try. He'll try his best. I'm sure of it.

TIM: Oh yeah, he'll do his best, but killing somebody; that's really big.

JANET: ...What were you teaching my daughter?

TIM: What would I teach her? I wasn't teaching.

JANET: This is a person with no knowledge. Anything would be helpful.

TIM: ...Really?

JANET: Sure. Teach her she doesn't have to be scared when the sun goes down because it comes back again tomorrow.

TIM: ...I can't teach her that.

JANET: Why not?

TIM: Because I don't *know* it.

JANET: Sure you do, I just told you. *(Picks up baby)* Can you show me the drain?

TIM: What drain?

JANET: Where the water goes out. I want to see where the water goes.

TIM: ...Outside?

JANET: Yes.

TIM: We can try.

Scene Seven

(The Jail. JANET, RUSSELL, THOMAS, *baby. Some discarded newspapers.* THOMAS *tries to explain things to* RUSSELL. *This is an explanation, not a memory.)*

THOMAS: I was fishing when the oil came. I knew something was wrong; the gulls, they were making terrible sounds, worse than usual. Suddenly, the boat was surrounded by black water. I leaned over the side and stuck a board in it, pulled it up. We knew what it was; the details we found out later. Janet was waiting at the dock; everybody was there. We didn't fish again. Everybody sat around and read the paper and drank beers—me too. We read their promises. "We will clean the mess. We will restore the coast." I got a job to clean the beach, but I didn't get a machine—a machine to suck oil. They gave me towels. Take these towels and wipe the rocks, they said. I thought they were special towels. I wiped a rock with a towel. The towel filled with oil and dirt and sand. I used another one. My towels didn't work. I took towels from one of the other guys; they didn't work either. It took me two hours and fifty towels to wipe a rock, and still, there was oil in the cracks. The rock wasn't clean. And there were thousands of rocks on the beach. I heard peeping; I looked around and saw a big gull flopping in the sand. I don't like gulls; they eat garbage and steal fish. Still, they're a part of the day. I went to it; it waddled in a circle, its wings covered with thick oil, peeping this little peep. I expected it to go away, they don't let you near. It didn't go away; it looked at me. I knelt down and peeped his peep at him. He came to me! I couldn't believe it. He came to me. "I can't help you, friend. I can't even clean a rock." ...I couldn't even clean a rock.

RUSSELL: ...How did you get to New York?

THOMAS: I hitchhiked and walked.

RUSSELL: And you had your gun?

THOMAS: Yeah.

RUSSELL: *(To* JANET*)* Did you know?

JANET: I suspected.

RUSSELL: What do you mean?

JANET: When the contract came we had a meeting.

RUSSELL: What contract?

JANET: Every town got a contract.

RUSSELL: From the oil company?

JANET: *(Nods)* The contract said we'd get money for lost fishing for three years.

RUSSELL: That doesn't sound so bad.

JANET: We would become subcontractors—so we couldn't say anything against the company. We couldn't talk to the government scientists, even to tell where the oil was beached.

THOMAS: They kept saying "the beaches are clean, the beaches are clean."

JANET: If we signed, there would be nobody to tell the truth.

RUSSELL: Could I see the contract?

JANET: *(Proudly)* We burned it.

THOMAS: *(Sarcastic)* That's right, Russell. We mustered our courage and set fire to the contract.

JANET: It showed we were united, Thomas.

THOMAS: United to do what? To burn a piece of paper? To haul dead seals to the dump?

JANET: To stand together.

THOMAS: To stand together while we died? While we were poisoned?

JANET: Some towns weren't united. At least we were.

THOMAS: I didn't think it was enough, Russell. Somehow, burning their contract was not enough for me. I wanted, oh, I don't know, a less symbolic act.

RUSSELL: ...Did you discuss it? Your act, at the meeting?

THOMAS: It wasn't even on T V anymore. Oil was still everywhere, and it wasn't on T V.

JANET: Thomas said his plan at the meeting. It was voted down.

RUSSELL: But nobody tried to stop you.

JANET: It was voted down.

THOMAS: It was impossible somebody would disobey.

RUSSELL: What was it supposed to accomplish?

THOMAS: It would be so violent that people would have to learn the reason for it. They would have to see where I come from—the T V people. They would have to show the beaches. At first, I thought I would kill myself like the monks in Viet Nam. But nobody cared about them. They wouldn't care about me, either.

RUSSELL: You could have killed the captain of the tanker. Why did you walk all the way across the country and kill the chairman of the board of directors?

THOMAS: *(Simply)* He told the most lies.

RUSSELL: ...How did you know he'd be in New York?

THOMAS: He's there sometimes. It just worked out.

Scene Eight

(A municipal building. TIM *and* JANET *holding baby)*

TIM: What do I say?

JANET: *(For the tenth time)* Tim. You ask for the map. That's all you have to do.

TIM: They're not going to give *me* anything.

JANET: Yes they will. Just do what we said.

TIM: Why can't you do it?

JANET: Because they are more likely to give it to you than to me, that's why.

TIM: Mom never makes me do stuff like this. She does stuff like this *for* me.

JANET: And you do this for *me*. So now it's even.

(They face front as an unseen functionary approaches.)

JANET: Just ask.

TIM: Hi. I'm here to get the plans of the city water system. It's for my science project. I have to show where the water comes from and where it goes. It's a big science...uh week. So I gotta have the map, okay? ...Her? She's, uh....

JANET: I'm his nanny.

TIM: Yeah! She's my nanny. For years. Since when I was a kid. Yeah.

Scene Nine

(The house. POLLY, RUSSELL, *his briefcase)*

RUSSELL: *(Chuckles)* The highway's blocked. I couldn't get through. There's animals on the road. Hundreds of them.

POLLY: What kind of animals?

RUSSELL: Sheep. Chickens. Goats and cows. It's really very noisy. Traffic in both directions is stopped.

POLLY: Is there a farmer?

RUSSELL: No. Just the animals. There's a pig with a lamb on its back.

POLLY: Russell.

RUSSELL: I saw it; a for-real piggy-back ride. I want to show Tim.

POLLY: He and Janet are playing somewhere.

RUSSELL: ...They sure spend a lot of time together.

POLLY: Tim adores her.

RUSSELL: They spend hours together. What do they do?

POLLY: They play.

RUSSELL: But it's hours, Polly. Hours.

POLLY: Well, maybe Janet *likes* playing with him, Russell.

RUSSELL: I like playing with him just fine, Polly.

POLLY: Then don't be astonished when somebody else likes it.

RUSSELL: He should play with his friends.

POLLY: There aren't any friends for him in this neighborhood.

RUSSELL: Don't start, Polly.

POLLY: There aren't any friends for me, either.

RUSSELL: Polly...

POLLY: And they're aren't any friends for you.

RUSSELL: People are perfectly friendly.

POLLY: Sure. A hello in the morning when we leave, a hi in the evening when we come home.

RUSSELL: What do you think, Polly? Do you think they're all getting together and having great evenings and not inviting us? Bridge games, poker parties, sipping beers around the V C R, Monday night football in front of the big-screen T V? And not inviting us black folks on the corner? Is that what you think?

POLLY: No, that's not what I think. I think they lock their door to *everybody*. I think they come home from work, bring in the children, seal off their homes, and turn on the answering machines. I think they're isolating themselves, and I think isolation is unhealthy.

(TIM enters with ball, bat, and glove.)

TIM: Dad! I thought you went to the office. You want to play ball? Catch?

RUSSELL: Have you been lonesome out here, Tim?

TIM: No. Janet plays with me. And there's always Sandy.

RUSSELL: *(To* POLLY*)* See? There's always Sandy.

TIM: Sandy's cool.

RUSSELL: And Sandy's cool.

TIM: How about it, Dad? Steee-riiike!

RUSSELL: I want to show you some sheep first.

TIM: Okay. I'll get Janet. *(Exits)*

RUSSELL: I guess we're *all* going to see sheep.

POLLY: I'll change my shoes.

Scene Ten

*(*JANET *and* POLLY *in the yard, digging with shovels)*

JANET: I had to scream louder because I was a breed from the city. I could never stay calm; I was so angry. My face would get red, I would shout, I would almost pop. It took me a long time to recognize that the bad guy is always calm. He calmly waits until I am done raving and then calmly refutes me with the biggest lies. Stupid onlookers nod in agreement. They respond to his calm, not his argument. I was so young.

POLLY: You're pretty young *now.*

JANET: No, really young, college. The campus activist. I spoke out, power to the people, justice-and-equality, back to the land, blah blah blah; boy, I didn't know anything.

POLLY: I think you're still an activist.

JANET: *(Mad)* Why do you say that? What makes you say that?

POLLY: Well, you're....

JANET: What, what am I?

POLLY: You seem ... to care, deeply.

(Pause, they dig.)

JANET: I don't think we're going to find the end of this root.

POLLY: I think you're right.

JANET: What is it?

POLLY: Some weed. It just showed up. It's clogging pipes all over town.

JANET: *(Quietly)* I'm not an activist. I *was* an activist. Me screaming into a crowd—the white man this and the white man that.

POLLY: *(Amused)* I made that speech.

JANET: Then you were an activist, too.

POLLY: Yep.

JANET: But not now, neither one of us.

POLLY: *(Brief pause)* It doesn't have to be a full-time job. You can make small stands every day. What you buy, what you watch on T V, what you listen to. Like that.

JANET: These small stands, is that what you meant when you made that speech?

POLLY: No, I meant bigger stands, I know that. But my life is different now; I still do what I can.

JANET: My life is different now, too. Now...I don't know.

POLLY: Russell says that you and Thomas don't always agree.

JANET: Yeah, Russell saw us fight. We fight all the time. I'm trying to turn him into me, he's trying to turn me into him. I guess we both succeeded.

POLLY: What do you mean?

JANET: I *have* turned into Thomas. I never noticed. He came to campus to hear the speeches. He listened to my big back-to-the-land speech. He asked me if I had ever lived without heat or electricity or running water. So I said my justice-and-equality speech. He listened the whole way, then he said, "So, what you're saying, Miss, is that we should stand up for our rights and get our piece of the pie. What I hear you saying, Miss, is that equal means we can have the right to destroy, chop down, level, and pollute, like our white brothers."

POLLY: Oh. ...He wanted you to be better than equal.

JANET: Right. Better. He was better. I wish I had noticed when he turned into me. Maybe I could have prevented this. *(Brief pause. She notices that* POLLY *looks troubled.)* What? Is that more than you wanted to know?

POLLY: No, I... *(Annoyed)* Russell hasn't turned into me at all.

JANET: Yes, but, you see, that's good. As long as you're you, there's no reason for him to be you, too.

Scene Eleven

(The house. TIM *wearing a bird mask, and* JANET*)*

TIM: They'd have a party?, a *party* to give their stuff away?!

JANET: To show off.

TIM: I don't get it. Okay, okay. A chief, a big chief puts his stuff in a pile, invites a lot of people over, and they take it away. Is that it?

JANET: I think so.

TIM: You *think*? Don't you know?

JANET: No.

TIM: You said you were an Indian.

JANET: Other tribes do it; not my one.

TIM: You never did it?

JANET: Not like this.

TIM: I think it's really stupid; giving your stuff away to show off. That's not how you show-off. That's how you show you're stupid. *You* think it's stupid, don't you?

JANET: *Showing off* is stupid.

TIM: No, *giving your stuff away* is stupid.

JANET: Let's do it.

TIM: *(Horrified)* You want me to give my stuff away?!

JANET: I'll give my stuff away.

TIM: You don't have any stuff.

JANET: I have a little bit of stuff. *(She takes a pen from her pocket and removes some jewelry, makes a pile.)* Welcome People. Welcome to my potlatch. I spread before you my jewels and my pen. Take what pleases you; scatter the rest to the wind.

TIM: Am I the People?

JANET: You be the People.

TIM: *(Big voice)* I take this necklace, and I take this bracelet; the pen I scatter to the winds.

JANET: I think you should take all my stuff or it's like an insult.

TIM: Okay, okay. *(Big voice)* I take the pen too.

JANET: And I am pleased to give it to you. Next year I hope you will come and clean me out again. ...What do you think?

TIM: I think it's really stupid. I got all your stuff, and I don't even like the pen.

JANET: *(Surprised)* I kinda liked it.

TIM: I got all your stuff!

JANET: But I feel okay about it.

TIM: *(Figuring it out)* Because you got to be *generous.*

JANET: Maybe that's it.

TIM: Yeah! That's *it*! They got to be generous.

Scene Twelve

(The court. RUSSELL *and* THOMAS, JANET *behind them)*

RUSSELL: We're not entering a plea of temporary insanity, your honor. I would be more inclined to enter a plea of temporary clarity of vision. ...I don't mean to offend the court. We're entering a plea of self-defense. ...Your honor, if you could see what's been done to this man's home and livelihood, you would see that his life *has been* threatened. ...I know who is on trial here, your Honor. ...No, your Honor, that is our plea. In the matter of bail for my client, your Honor, ...but your Honor. Yes, I know the severity of the charge, but... how can you expect this man to raise that amount of money?

THOMAS: They don't expect me to. They don't want me to. I can touch the walls. *(He extends his arms as if touching both jail cell walls.)*

Scene Thirteen

(The house. POLLY *wiping up floor with paper towels.* RUSSELL *and* JANET *enter.)*

POLLY: Russell, help me.

RUSSELL: What a mess.

POLLY: I know it's a mess, thank you. I'm trying to stop it before it gets behind the baseboards.

JANET: Not with towels. *(Exits)*

RUSSELL: This is hopeless.

POLLY: It's spreading over there, Russell.

RUSSELL: How did you *do* this, Polly?

POLLY: It slipped out of my hand. You're standing in it.

RUSSELL: I can't help it, it's everywhere.

POLLY: Then at at least take off your shoes.

RUSSELL: So I can wipe it up with my socks?

*(*JANET *enters with dirt and dumps it on the floor.)*

JANET: Here you go.

*(*RUSSELL *and* POLLY *are stunned.)*

JANET: Get out of the way, Polly. *(Spreads dirt on floor)* They do this on the roads when oil trucks turn over. Move, Russell.

RUSSELL: *(Sarcastic)* Good thing you didn't do this on the living room rug, Polly.

JANET: Yes. It would have ruined the rug.

RUSSELL: And it may ruin the tile.

JANET: What's wrong? Oh, you have an opinion about the dirt. Look, look at it. See? It's coming up. I know about this. I'm a sort of expert on this.

POLLY: *(To* RUSSELL*)* It *is* coming up.

RUSSELL: You should have asked, or explained, at least.

JANET: I didn't think it would be a big deal.

RUSSELL: Think next time, okay?

POLLY: Russell, it's coming up.

RUSSELL: You can't dump dirt in a house.

JANET: I was trying to help. I'll clean it up. *(Amused)* Then I'll take my savage and primitive self to my room.

RUSSELL: I can't say anything anymore. Everything turns into a thing.

(Brief pause. POLLY *notices that they are edgy.)*

POLLY: How did it go today?

JANET: Excellent.

RUSSELL: *(At the same time)* Horrible.

JANET: It was excellent. You should hear Russell *talk.*

RUSSELL: We didn't get bail.

JANET: We got bail. We can't pay it is all.

RUSSELL: I expected to get reasonable bail.

JANET: Well, some of us didn't expect to.

POLLY: It was on the national news.

JANET: Did they show the beaches?!

POLLY: No. They reenacted the crime with actors.

Scene Fourteen

(The house. RUSSELL, POLLY *with a newspaper)*

RUSSELL: *(Amazed)* Both of them think so. If the oil spill is on T V, everything will change. A wave of morality will cross the nation. The public will rise in indignation and demand restitution for the land. Oil tankers will be banned from the ocean, solar energy will fuel the future.

POLLY: It isn't even in the paper anymore.

RUSSELL: No?

POLLY: Replaced by the gooney birds.

RUSSELL: The what?

POLLY: Gooney birds on Midway Island.

RUSSELL: What are you talking about?

POLLY: On the front page. Haven't you seen the paper?

RUSSELL: No. I'm not...current.

POLLY: You certainly aren't. Gooneys are nesting on the runways on Midway Island. The planes can't take off.

RUSSELL: Why doesn't somebody shoo them away?

POLLY: Apparently they won't shoo.

RUSSELL: They won't shoo. *(Sigh)* This case is making me feel—I don't know.

POLLY: Useless.

RUSSELL: No.

POLLY: Stupid.

RUSSELL: No!

POLLY: Well, what's the word?

RUSSELL: I don't know.

POLLY: *(Brief pause)* Civilized?

RUSSELL: Too civilized... I don't know.

POLLY: ...Russell, I don't *want* to stop bleaching the laundry.

RUSSELL: Okaaay.

POLLY: Every time I do anything, she's looking at me. I am not a bad person because I like clean clothes.

RUSSELL: I know. ...Do you want her to leave?

POLLY: No. ...I just want to know the word for somebody who likes clean clothes.

RUSSELL: *(Quietly)* Thank you. It's going to get worse for her when the trial starts.

POLLY: Why?

RUSSELL: He's guilty, Polly. He's guilty of premeditated murder.

POLLY: Russell. Do you believe what you say at home, or do you believe what you say in court?

RUSSELL: You know how it is.

POLLY: No, I find it confusing. I prefer what you say in court. I guess if I preferred what you say at home, I'd understand.

Scene Fifteen

(The house. TIM *in bird mask.* TIM *"flies," makes bird sounds, and then talks to the People.)*

TIM: Welcome People, welcome to my potluck. Tonight I give you my sacred stuff. You can do with it what you feel like doing with it, it'll be yours. I give *you* my bike, and I give *you* my football and pads, I give *you* my baseball bat and glove, I give *you* my books and comic collection, I give *you* all my money.

*(*SANDY *enters. Her fabulous wings are visible for the first time.)*

SANDY: What will you give to me?

TIM: Wow. Great outfit.

SANDY: Thank you.

TIM: I don't know that outfit.

SANDY: Sure you do.

TIM: To Sandy I give, what's left? I give you all my baseball cards, both boxes.

SANDY: *(Dances)* Thank you. You are very generous.

*(*TIM *follows dancing.)*

SANDY: What will you keep for yourself?

TIM: I'm gonna keep my mask! Nobody's gonna get my mask.

*(*TIM *and* SANDY *dance.)*

Scene Sixteen

(The yard. JANET, *baby. The story* JANET *will tell if* THOMAS *isn't freed.)*

JANET: *(To baby)* Long ago the people of the world were blinded by a terrible curse. A rich evil man kept the curse locked in a strongbox. As long as he owned the curse, everybody would be kept in blindness, filth, and poverty. As the evil man stole from the helpless blind people, his heart beat louder. Each time he stole, the noise from within his chest grew, until it deafened the land. A brave blind man followed the sound to the castle of the evil rich man. The good man found the counting room where he killed the evil one and released the curse. The blind were healed. Gold coins turned into water and flooded the land. Crops grew and the people tilled the soil. To this day, the good man remains vigilant in the watch tower, keeping the evil ones away.

Scene Seventeen

(The house. RUSSELL *with a bat and ball)*

RUSSELL: Hey! Hey, Tim. *(To himself)* I hope I remember how to do this.

(Enter TIM *in bird mask.)*

RUSSELL: You can't play ball in that.

TIM: ...We're going to play ball?

RUSSELL: We are indeed.

TIM: ...We're gonna use that stuff?

RUSSELL: We're gonna use this stuff.

TIM: Oh, man. I don't know.

RUSSELL: Hey, you've been on me to play, now I got some time, let's *play ball.*

TIM: ...I can't play with that stuff anymore.

RUSSELL: Tim, we just got this stuff. You can't be bored with this already.

TIM: I can't play with it anymore, Dad.

RUSSELL: Well, I'll have to go out and find somebody else to play ball with me.

TIM: *You* can't play with it either, Dad.

RUSSELL: Yep, me and some other little boy.

TIM: *Dad*! You can't, you can't. You really can't, Dad.

RUSSELL: Take off that mask, will you, please. Why can't I, why can't we play with this?

TIM: It's not mine to use anymore. I don't think it's yours either.

RUSSELL: *(Breath)* It's mine, it's in my house, I can use it.

TIM: I gave it away. It's not ours anymore.

RUSSELL: Why is it still here, if you gave it away?

TIM: It's still here because it's just temporarily here.

RUSSELL: Take off the mask. Take it off.

*(*TIM *does.)*

RUSSELL: Don't you want to play, Tim?

TIM: Dad. Dad. *Dad*. I *want* to play. I gotta put these away. Let go.

*(*RUSSELL *lets go;* TIM *exits with stuff.)*

RUSSELL: *(Pause)* Polly!

*(*POLLY *enters)*

RUSSELL: What is going on? What is going on?

POLLY: What?

RUSSELL: I pick up a bat and ball, a recently purchased bat and ball, planning a little infield practice with my son, who informs me that said bat and ball are no longer his. Are, in fact, no longer *ours,* even though they are residing in our house, they are not *ours.*

POLLY: Oh. I noticed Tim had arranged his things. His things are in a very peculiar arrangement. Piles. Neat piles. That's why I didn't say anything. It was so neat, I didn't feel I had the moral high ground from which to complain.

RUSSELL: ...I don't think this is funny, Polly.

POLLY: I see that.

RUSSELL: Do you know who he gave his bat and ball to?

POLLY: It's just a game.

RUSSELL: A game? Why doesn't he play cowboys and Indians like other little boys?

POLLY: Because other little boys don't play cowboys and Indians. Not for years, Russell.

RUSSELL: ...Why do you have to turn everything into a thing?

POLLY: *(Happy)* It's my job. If I didn't, you'd have to.

RUSSELL: ...Why can't I play baseball with my son?

POLLY: Maybe you could play something else with him.

RUSSELL: I don't know how to play anything else.

POLLY: Maybe he'll teach you something.

Scene Eighteen

(The house. RUSSELL, TIM *in bird mask,* SANDY*)*

TIM: Yeah, okay. Okay. You say to the People what you're going to give away. You put your stuff in piles, and then it goes away.

RUSSELL: *(Referring to* SANDY*)* And you got that? In trade?

TIM: Dad, Dad, Dad. Do you want to try it?

RUSSELL: I don't know about this, Tim.

TIM: You want to watch me do it? I could do it first.

RUSSELL: I don't think you have anything left.

TIM: Yeah, I do. *(He takes off necklace, puts it on ground.)*

RUSSELL: Where'd you get that? Isn't that Janet's?

TIM: Dad. It's mine. I got it. It's fine. *(Pulls on mask)* I give my sacred necklace to the People. Take it if it pleases you, or scatter it to the winds.

RUSSELL: Now what?

TIM: It'll go away.

RUSSELL: By itself?

TIM: Dad, it's going to go away. You want to try it?

RUSSELL: Okay.

TIM: Here, put this on. *(Bird mask)*

RUSSELL: Did you get this from Janet?

TIM: Yeah. Now, Dad, don't fool around. This is *big*. Don't give stuff away that you still want, because it's gotta go when you give it away.

RUSSELL: Do I have to go get it?

TIM: Just say what it is; you can get it later.

RUSSELL: Who am I giving it to?

TIM: To the People.

RUSSELL: Okay. I give my old suit to the People.

TIM: *(Exasperated)* Mom took your old suit to the shelter.

RUSSELL: When did she do that?

TIM: Last week. Me and Janet and Mom packed up all our good old stuff and took it into town.

RUSSELL: *(Indignant)* What else did she take?

TIM: She took your old tan shoes.

RUSSELL: There wasn't anything wrong with those shoes!

TIM: There wasn't anything wrong with *anything*. We took *good* stuff. Bad stuff we cut up.

RUSSELL: Cut up for what?

TIM: For stuff. Give away your golf clubs.

RUSSELL: I've never used them.

TIM: Yeah, and you're never going to.

RUSSELL: ...I give away my golf clubs.

TIM: *(Big voice)* My *sacred* golf clubs. To the People.

RUSSELL: I give away my sacred golf clubs to the People.

Scene Nineteen

(The house. TIM, JANET, SANDY. *Maps and blueprints.* TIM *speaks into phone,* JANET *is aware of* SANDY.*)*

TIM: *(On phone)* Hi, I'm doing a big science project about the water and sewer system. Yeah, for my school. I'm making a model. Okay. *(To* JANET*)* They're connecting me to public relations.

JANET: Hey, why not? You're the public.

TIM: What should I ask?

JANET: Ask where the treatment station is for this sector. *(Points to map).*

TIM: *(Into phone)* Hi! ...Yeah, I'm doing a science project for school. ...Timmy, Tim. ...I'm *ten*. ...Okay, okay. I got a big map of the sewer system already, and now I'm making a model. What I need to know is, where is the treatment station for sector 455 on blueprint number *(Reading from map)* LI-334021. ...LI-334021. *(To* JANET*)* I'm on hold again. Hi...there isn't one?

JANET: *(Whispers)* What happens to the waste?

TIM: Where does the waste go? ...The ocean.

Scene Twenty

(The house. SANDY, POLLY. POLLY *looks at* SANDY. *Then* RUSSELL *enters with an envelope.)*

RUSSELL: Could you translate this for me? *(Hands* POLLY *letter)* I looked up that tribe—those "cool" guys that give all their stuff away. You know anything about those guys?

POLLY: Not much.

RUSSELL: Well, they weren't exactly perfect; they had feuds and wars, they turned captured prisoners into slaves. They were not perfect people, Polly.

POLLY: This is some letter, Russell.

RUSSELL: It came with a big check for Thomas's defense. ...What's that—that totem-thing doing in here?

POLLY: I don't know.

RUSSELL: Tim should keep his things in his room.

POLLY: He says it isn't his.

RUSSELL: That's convenient.

POLLY: He says it isn't his, Russell.

*(*RUSSELL *looks closely at* SANDY.*)*

RUSSELL: Where did this *come* from?

POLLY: I don't know. Looks pretty authentic.

RUSSELL: Janet didn't have this when I picked her up at the airport. Did somebody deliver it?

POLLY: Ask Tim. Russell, is something wrong?

RUSSELL: This face, this very female face, this beautiful face, it looks like you.

POLLY: No it doesn't.

RUSSELL: I think so.

POLLY: It looks...like you. I don't know why I didn't notice it before.

RUSSELL: It doesn't look anything like me. It's beautiful.

POLLY: It looks like you to me.

RUSSELL: Well. Thanks. ...Um, what's the letter?

POLLY: Monsieur—

RUSSELL: I got that far.

POLLY: Monsieur. We read of the final justice as it begins on your vast shores. Death met by death. No longer can they hide behind their thick corporate walls. The truth slips through the barricades to mete out its sentence. The walls come tumbling down.

RUSSELL: Welcome to the idiot fringe.

Scene Twenty-one

(A shore along the Long Island Sound. Gull noises. JANET *and* TIM *approach, looking up at birds.)*

JANET: Seagulls eat anything. Thomas doesn't like them.

TIM: Then I don't like them either.

JANET: I do. Lots of different kinds; an extended family.

*(*TIM *looks toward the water.)*

TIM: Is that it?

JANET: Where?

TIM: That pipe. Sticking out of the rocks.

JANET: I think so.

TIM: What's that stuff in the water?

JANET: What do you think!

TIM: Do you think any of it's from our house?

JANET: I don't know—does any of it look familiar?

(A shadow passes over them. They look up.)

TIM: Wow. What kind of bird is that?

JANET: *(Amazed)* It's an eagle. I didn't think they had them here. Do they have them here?

TIM: Sure. There's one now.

(The shadow passes over again. They watch silently. Then JANET *puts stones in a pile.)*

JANET: Give me a hand.

TIM: ...What are you doing?

JANET: Piling stones.

TIM: Why?

JANET: I need your help.

TIM: This is heavy.

JANET: That's why you gotta help.

TIM: What's it *for*?

JANET: ...So somebody can find this place, I don't know. Help me.

Scene Twenty-two

(The house. RUSSELL, JANET *completing a homemade doll,* SANDY.*)*

RUSSELL: Tim is getting...very confused.

JANET: I don't think so.

RUSSELL: Yes, he's developing an irresponsible relationship to his things. He's been taught to appreciate and take care of his things. I want him to continue to do that.

JANET: Okay.

RUSSELL: Taking care of his things doesn't make him a bad person. It's responsible.

JANET: Sure.

RUSSELL: He gets a thing, he takes care of it, he keeps it for a while, and in good time he throws it away.

JANET: Maybe he shouldn't throw it away. It might be useful.

RUSSELL: I'm sure it *is* useful; he's throwing everything away.

JANET: What's he throwing away?

RUSSELL: Everything. All his toys, gone. It's got to stop.

JANET: Tim doesn't throw his toys away.

RUSSELL: Yes, to the winds, or something.

JANET: He takes his toys to the shelter and gives them to the kids.

RUSSELL: Oh. I didn't know.

JANET: Yes, it's very generous.

RUSSELL: Is that where my golf clubs went?

JANET: No, your golf clubs we sold.

RUSSELL: You *sold* my golf clubs?

JANET: Yes; we got seventy dollars. I didn't know they were worth so much.

RUSSELL: They're worth.... *(Sigh)* What did you do with the money?

JANET: Tim. I think he gave it to the poor.

RUSSELL: Which poor?

JANET: I don't know which. We see a lot of poor.

RUSSELL: I don't—I don't—I don't think he should play with these totem things.

JANET: What totem things?

RUSSELL: *(SANDY)* That, that!

JANET: That's not a totem, Russell.

RUSSELL: Whatever it is, whatever you call it, it's not Tim's heritage. I don't want him to be confused about how to be.

JANET: There's different ways he can be.

RUSSELL: I want him to be a successful, professional something. I want him to contribute to society.

JANET: Maybe Tim doesn't want to contribute to society.

RUSSELL: That's what I'm talking about! That's exactly what I'm talking about! I am part of this country, and my son is part of this country.

JANET: And its heritage is your heritage.

RUSSELL: Yes, it is. Tim is an American.

JANET: And what am I?

RUSSELL: I don't know what you are.

JANET: I know you don't. You think we're just kidding. That we're going to come to our senses one day and stop being Indians. That's what you white people think. That as soon as we grow up, we'll want our share of the spoils.

RUSSELL: You white people?

JANET: *(Blustering)* Thomas walked across the country on a mission. Misguided, maybe, but he *walked* across the country. Or maybe you think because he got some rides, it isn't a big deal—

RUSSELL: Of course it's a big deal—

JANET: We stand at the edge of the reservation and ask why is this side different from that side? Nothing is like it ought to be. Life is tough for us, Russell, and the oil, that was the last straw. Thomas killed somebody; some of our friends killed themselves. Why isn't that on T V?

RUSSELL: ...I don't know.

(A silence. They are sad. TIM *enters.)*

TIM: Hey, Dad. Hey, Janet. Wow, where did you get that? *(Doll)*

JANET: I made it.

TIM: Oh yeah, there's my old shirt. Who's it for?

JANET: It's for someone who'll love it.

TIM: I love it.

JANET: I guess it's for you, then.

TIM: Great. Thanks. Thanks a lot. *(He exits with doll.)*

RUSSELL: Will he give it away?

JANET: I don't know. It's okay if he does.

Scene Twenty-three

(Jail. RUSSELL *and* THOMAS. *A newspaper)*

THOMAS: Why do you have to understand?

RUSSELL: I can't make a jury understand, I can't make a judge understand, unless I understand. Unless I understand fully.

THOMAS: You didn't need to understand my state of mind before; you just needed to know what happened.

RUSSELL: Well, I need to *now*, so you better take a few minutes to explain it to me, okay?

THOMAS: I don't know how.

RUSSELL: ...I'm trying to get at, or invent, the key to our defense. I need to know every detail. I don't mean to annoy you.

THOMAS: I walked across the country. I got a lot of rides.

RUSSELL: How did you wash? How did you eat? Did you hunt for food?

THOMAS: *(Amused)* I ate in restaurants, Russell.

RUSSELL: I...I'm sorry.

THOMAS: *(Laughs)* Okay, Russell, calm down. *(Big breath)* I washed in gas stations. After a while the towns become one big town, and the gas stations lock their toilets. People are less friendly. I stayed dirty. I got fewer rides.

RUSSELL: Tell me about your state of mind.

THOMAS: I don't know *how* to tell about a state of mind.

RUSSELL: Okay, okay. Just *talk* to me.

THOMAS: I decided to kill him, and then I started my trip. The whole time I was on the road I'd try to think about it. I'd decide to think about it, and then all of a sudden I'd be thinking of something else. It was hard to think about it. Is that a state of mind? ...When I got to New York, I cleaned up and changed into the costume. The great warrior. I told the woman I was there for the American heritage live-diorama, and she let me pass. *(Chuckles)* "Live-diorama." On the trip, someone said, where are you going? When I said New York, he said, oh don't miss the Museum of Natural History's Indian dioramas.

RUSSELL: They fired her.

THOMAS: The woman who let me pass?

RUSSELL: Yes. ...Thomas, this crime is very premeditated.

THOMAS: As much as I could.

RUSSELL: That's very bad.

THOMAS: No. To do it thoughtlessly would be very bad.

*(*RUSSELL *doesn't know what to say; sighs, picks up the newspaper, reads, then.)*

RUSSELL: What is this? *(Excited)* What?!

THOMAS: It's my paper.

RUSSELL: Thomas. ...Thomas. This is great. This is great for us, look at this. *(reading)* Oh boy it's a different story when it happens in your own backyard.

THOMAS: It's all one country.

RUSSELL: Thomas, to New Yorkers, America is *New York*. To New Yorkers, Americans are *New Yorkers*. And it's downright un-American to spoil their beaches.

THOMAS: I understand that.

RUSSELL: There's tar balls from Long Beach to East Hampton. The Mayor's planning a law suit; the governor's going on T V tonight. Did you read this?

THOMAS: I read it, Russell.

RUSSELL: Did you see these pictures? Black sea gulls, a grimy puppy.

THOMAS: I read it, *and* I looked at the pictures.

RUSSELL: Thomas, this is the city of the media. Nobody's going to stop the story of *this* spill. This will stay in the news until every drop of oil is off the beach. And people here are going to have to see *you* in a new light; when they talk about you, they're going to be a little gentler. They're going to understand your outrage because they're feeling it themselves. This is great. I predict reasonable bail by the end of the week.

THOMAS: Very reasonable—it only cost a coastline.

Scene Twenty-four

(The house. TIM *coming out of the vent,* SANDY*)*

TIM: The vents are like being inside an animal.

SANDY: You're pretty dirty.

TIM: *(Cleaning up)* Yeah, I got my towel. It's like crawling down his throat into his stomach.

SANDY: Her stomach.

TIM: Yeah. Listening to the beats.

SANDY: *(Dances)* Moving in time to the beats. Careful not to disrupt.
Add to the music, your own special sound.

TIM: Don't poke her in the side or else she'll bleed.

SANDY: And if she dies...

TIM: Then we'll die with her.

(They dance. Fade to black as sound of sea rises)

END OF ACT ONE

ACT TWO

Scene One

(The house. TIM *with a picture,* SANDY, *and* THOMAS*)*

TIM: They let you out.

THOMAS: For now, yes.

TIM: I did this.

THOMAS: Show me.

*(*TIM *shows* THOMAS *the picture. The picture makes* THOMAS *really happy.)*

THOMAS: It's beautiful.

TIM: No. I should spend more time on a picture.

THOMAS: This one didn't take more time?

TIM: A couple of minutes is all.

THOMAS: It has a great—...I don't know how to say it.

TIM: *(Sensing a compliment)* Could you try?

THOMAS: Something like "gentleness."

TIM: *(Happy)* How long are you going to live with us?

THOMAS: Until I get a job. Your father doesn't think anybody will give me one.

TIM: Maybe you should just stay. Janet's happy now.

THOMAS: She was sad?

TIM: Yeah. But not anymore. If you stay, you could teach me how to kill them—

THOMAS: But—

TIM: And I could teach you how to paint in exchange.

THOMAS: I would like to learn to paint, but Tim, I can't teach—

TIM: Sure you can.

*(*RUSSELL *enters with paper.)*

RUSSELL: Thomas, did you want the paper?

TIM: Dad, I painted this.

RUSSELL: Tim's sort of the artist in the family. Nice. Did you spend a lot of time on it?

TIM: Oh, Dad. It didn't take any time at all. It sort of came to me whole, in a message.

RUSSELL: Oh. What's the message?

TIM: I can't tell you.

RUSSELL: Secret?

TIM: No. It's not English.

RUSSELL: What language is it?

TIM: I don't think it's language. It's a message.

RUSSELL: Code?

TIM: Sort of code.

THOMAS: I used to hear messages.

TIM: I don't *hear* them, I *see* them.

THOMAS: I heard mine.

RUSSELL: *(Worried)* You still getting messages?

THOMAS: No. Now I read newspapers.

TIM: Do you get messages, Dad?

RUSSELL: *(Getting intense)* No. No messages. Just studying, learning, figuring it out. Unfortunately, I had to do it the hard way. It didn't come to me in messages.

TIM: Dad, Dad. What are you talking about?

RUSSELL: That I fought hard, and studied hard to learn the things that I know. They didn't come to me in messages.

TIM: But Dad, I study. I have to work hard to learn stuff. This isn't the same as that.

RUSSELL: The stuff that you learn; that's all there is. There are no messages. Excuse me. *(Exits)*

THOMAS: Maybe your father is right.

TIM: How can he be right? I *got* this message.

(Enter POLLY.*)*

POLLY: Tim. *(To* THOMAS, *uncomfortable)* Hello.

TIM: I did this, Mom.

POLLY: Yes, it's very nice, Tim.

TIM: You didn't look at it.

POLLY: It's nice. You're very talented. Come on, Tim, let's find Dad.

TIM: Why?

POLLY: Come on, let's go.

*(*POLLY *and* TIM *exit.* THOMAS *looks at* SANDY.*)*

Scene Two

*(*THOMAS, SANDY, JANET, *baby, in the yard)*

JANET: Everything is so fast here.

THOMAS: Yeah. It's fast, it's loud, nobody listens.

JANET: Polly listens. She's my friend.

THOMAS: She's afraid of me.

JANET: I don't think so.

THOMAS: *(Considers it)* Maybe you're right. They let us stay in their house.

JANET: Yes.

THOMAS: Someday they can stay in our house.

JANET: We don't have a house.

THOMAS: What happened to our house?

JANET: We can't go back.

THOMAS: They're mad I shot that guy?

JANET: Not so much. They're mad you went against the decision.

THOMAS: *(Brief pause)* I always heard a sound; like things were talking in my mind. When I decided to kill that man, the sound stopped. I told myself it would start again after I shot him. I wanted to kill him, so I tricked myself. It was never right. ...I hurt you.

JANET: You made me mad. You put yourself above the decision, and you put everybody else in danger. The white man's revenge is never even-steven. We were afraid to go to sleep at night.

THOMAS: The cavalry doesn't ride up and burn villages anymore.

JANET: And men don't settle things with guns?

THOMAS: You are...you are so....

JANET: What?

THOMAS: I don't know what it's called. Everything is simple for you.

JANET: Not so simple.

THOMAS: Yes. You were an activist and that was everything. There was nothing else. It was clear. Then all of a sudden you were a wife and not an activist and that was clear. You lived in a town, then you lived at a college, then you lived on a reservation, and now you live in Russell's house. It's always clear, always simple.

JANET: I help them clean up.

THOMAS: You help them clean up, just like that, like you always did it.

JANET: No, we had to work it out. It wasn't simple.

THOMAS: We don't *live* here.

JANET: We live here *now.*

THOMAS: This isn't our house.

JANET: But it's okay if we stay.

THOMAS: *(Exasperated)* Maybe they'll let *you* come back.

JANET: I won't go. I came here to help you.

THOMAS: Help me what? I did what I did and now there's nothing to help.

JANET: I can help you change back.

THOMAS: I can't change any more.

JANET: People change until they're dead.

THOMAS: That man I shot—

JANET: He's dead, can't change—

THOMAS: People like that don't change—

JANET: Not once they're dead!

THOMAS: *(Sigh, pause)* I don't know anything; there's only silence.

JANET: Try to listen again—try to open up. *(Joking)* Don't do it in the subway, though.

Scene Three

(The house. POLLY, *water glass,* SANDY. *Enter* RUSSELL.*)*

POLLY: Look.

RUSSELL: What is it?

POLLY: It's water. It's filthy. It's from the tap.

RUSSELL: Don't drink it.

POLLY: I'm not going to drink it.

RUSSELL: Is there anything about it on the radio?

POLLY: No.

RUSSELL: Where's the family?

POLLY: They're standing on the ground.

RUSSELL: The ground?

POLLY: Yes. They're standing on the ground. They're standing on the ground and thinking about it. Thomas missed the ground when he was in prison. He's visiting the ground.

RUSSELL: Where's Tim?

POLLY: Standing on the ground.

RUSSELL: Polly!

POLLY: What?! What do you want me to say?

RUSSELL: I want you to look after our son.

POLLY: You want me to keep him on the sidewalk? Keep him on the cement? Because that's what it's going to take. You're going to have to keep him on the cement or he's going to visit the ground, and once he has, nothing you or I or anybody else says is going to make him unknow what he learns from her.

RUSSELL: Polly—...it's ground. It's sand. It's grass. It's roots, it's coal mines and gravel pits. It's not a her.

POLLY: I don't think so. I don't think you're right, Russell.

RUSSELL: Well, I think I am.

POLLY: What about the rocks?

RUSSELL: I don't know about rocks.

POLLY: Piles of rocks everywhere; it was on T V.

RUSSELL: It's probably just...art.

Scene Four

(The house. RUSSELL, SANDY. RUSSELL *stares at* SANDY *for a moment. Looks around, almost says something. Doesn't. Exits)*

Scene Five

(The house. THOMAS, RUSSELL, SANDY*)*

RUSSELL: We're all born into this civilization. We don't ask for it. We grow up, we look around, and it's a mess. What do we do? Do we stand there and whine about it? No. We pull ourselves up by the bootstraps.

THOMAS: I had a lot to overcome.

RUSSELL: I know, I know, I'm not saying you didn't, I know you did, but listen. Listen. What if everybody stood around waiting for messages?

THOMAS: Nobody's waiting, they just come.

RUSSELL: If you stand around waiting for a message, you're not going to get anything done. You won't help yourself out of the mire. You become part of the idiot fringe. It's like—astrology, or science fiction movies where the aliens have all the answers, or conspiracy theories, or waiting for judgment day.

THOMAS: The idiot fringe isn't all idiots.

RUSSELL: You can't stand around and talk to a whatever-you-call-it—... Totem Pole and expect anything to get straight.

THOMAS: *(Brief pause)* You tried it?

RUSSELL: Tried what?

THOMAS: Talking to the... *(Points to* SANDY*)*

RUSSELL: No. Talking to inanimate objects is just talking to yourself.

THOMAS: Talking to myself is a good thing. I can't fool myself; when I talk to myself, it's always honest.

RUSSELL: I'm not having trouble with honesty, Thomas.

THOMAS: I meant when *I* have trouble with honesty, not when *you* have trouble with honesty. ...Russell, when is something going to happen? I don't like this waiting.

RUSSELL: Time is good for us. Every time there's one of these little things in the paper, the public sentiment shifts our way. The syringes on the beaches.

THOMAS: That's not little.

RUSSELL: The toxic pile on Staten Island, this sewage scandal right in our own neighborhood.

THOMAS: These things that are really good for me are making me feel really bad. I don't want to wait any more.

RUSSELL: ...There's been a delay.

THOMAS: Did you ask for a delay?

RUSSELL: This doesn't have anything to do with me. Or you. It's a computer problem. Rats got into the mainframe. Ate some chips, something. It's a mess.

THOMAS: Why do I have a delay because of that?

RUSSELL: Everything's on the computer. The court schedule; everything. Nothing's happening in court until they get the network up again. They hired a consultant.

THOMAS: Maybe this isn't a computer problem. Maybe this is a rat problem.

Scene Six

(The house. JANET, SANDY. *A pile of rocks,* POLLY *enters.)*

POLLY: What's that?

JANET: A marker. To mark the troubled water from the tap.

POLLY: I *knew* it was you.

JANET: Me and Tim have been building them where it's appropriate.

POLLY: I knew but I don't think I knew I knew. ...Listen to me talk— I've stopped making sense.

JANET: I understood.

POLLY: Tim didn't say anything about it.

JANET: There's not much to say.

POLLY: Did somebody drive you around?

JANET: Nobody drove.

POLLY: You couldn't have walked to the Hamptons.

JANET: We took a train to the Hamptons, and then we walked.

POLLY: What's supposed to happen now? Are these rocks going to give me clean water when I turn on the tap?

JANET: I'm taking a stand. Like you said.

POLLY: *(Speechless)* When you take a stand you refuse to purchase something. That's a stand. Hurt a company, and they change their policy.

JANET: How do they even know you're doing it?

POLLY: *(Losing control)* Because they *know* it, I do it with *others*. We write a *letter*. It *works*. It's *financial*. Oh, boy.

JANET: People want to see the stones; they go to see them, they have to look at the sewage.

POLLY: What's it supposed to accomplish? What you're doing, it's not really *doing* anything, it's just so *somebody else* does something.

JANET: That's all doing is, so somebody else does something. You boycott companies in South Africa, I pile stones. Thomas killed a man.

POLLY: That's not the same thing.

JANET: It was supposed to be.

(Enter RUSSELL*)*

RUSSELL: What's going...what's that? Where did these rocks come from?

JANET: I brought them.

RUSSELL: Janet! Did you build the rock piles?

JANET: Me and Tim.

RUSSELL: Tim? *My* Tim? Some of those places are dangerous.

JANET: All of them are dangerous.

RUSSELL: There's hundreds of them.

JANET: We only built nine.

RUSSELL: Where did the rest of them come from? Are you going to tell me they just sprang up, out of the *earth*, out of the *ground*?

JANET: Other people built them, Russell. There's lots of places where they ought to be built. Me and Tim can't do it all.

RUSSELL: What about the ones downtown?

JANET: Other people.

RUSSELL: At City Hall.

JANET: We didn't do those.

RUSSELL: Have you been talking about this?

JANET: We don't talk—we pile stones.

RUSSELL: Don't...build any more, and don't take Tim with you.

Scene Seven

(The house. POLLY *and* SANDY, *rocks.* POLLY *is on her way to work, looks at a vocabulary list, says aloud "drift net fishing." Looks at another list, says "la filet derivante," pause, then:)*

POLLY: *(To* SANDY*)* When I learned French, in the beginning, I was outside of French, looking at it, touching it, remembering each word next to its English sister. I was a walking English-French Dictionary. Each French word was a temporary and flimsy substitute for the *real* word which was, of course, the English word. I became fluent in French, except for the French words for which there is no English equivalent. *Those* words, those untranslatable words, came slower, but settled in with an undeniable permanence. They defined me. I pulled them on like a mask. Then there came the dreams, the dreams I dreamt in French. I'd wake up not knowing what the words meant, not knowing if I'd used them properly in the dream. *(Pause. Silence. She puts a stone on the pile, not looking at* SANDY.*)* When I dream about you, when we speak in the dream, I don't understand the language at all. *(As if engulfed)* Oh, yes. Oh, yes.

Scene Eight

(The house. RUSSELL, TIM *with papers,* SANDY, *rocks)*

RUSSELL: What're you doing, Tim?

TIM: *(Furious)* Math.

RUSSELL: I was good at math.

TIM: I was, too. Until this part.

RUSSELL: What is it?

TIM: Positive and negative numbers.

RUSSELL: I sort of remember those.

TIM: Everybody sort of remembers them, but nobody really remembers them because they don't make any sense.

RUSSELL: They make sense.

TIM: *(Explodes)* Sea Level!

RUSSELL: What about it?

TIM: Above sea level is positive and below sea level is negative, but what if the ocean rises?

RUSSELL: That's not going to happen.

TIM: It will if the ice caps melt! They haven't figured this out; it doesn't make sense.

RUSSELL: Let me take a look at that. It's all right here, Tim. When you add two positives you add; when you add two negatives you add; when you add a positive and a negative you subtract. When you subtract two negatives you add; when you multiply two positives it's positive; when you multiply two negatives it's positive; when you multiply a positive and a negative it's—

TIM: Stop it, stop it! Why would I want to multiply a positive and a negative. Where is this negative? It doesn't exist. It's under water.

RUSSELL: Maybe you have to memorize it—maybe you'll understand it later.

TIM: It's a trick. I'll memorize it, then they'll change the rules and I'll fail the test.

RUSSELL: This isn't a conspiracy against you, Tim. Stop taking your flaws personally.

TIM: What?!

RUSSELL: You should *focus.* Make yourself understand it.

TIM: Dad, Dad, Dad. You don't even use them. You said you only sort of remember them, so you can't be using them.

RUSSELL: *(A calmness that presages hysteria)* If you don't make yourself understand this, a little bit at a time, then you aren't going to be able to understand calculus when it comes along. It'll be hieroglyphics to you.

TIM: *(Frightened)* What are those?

RUSSELL: *(Deadly focus)* You got to wrestle with it all the way. It will make sense if you can only keep up with it one step at a time.

TIM: I'm not going to give up, Dad.

RUSSELL: If you can just keep at it, it can't overwhelm you.

TIM: Yes it can.

RUSSELL: If you keep paying attention, and don't turn a blind eye to the stuff as it mounts up, this way, it's just a little bit at a time. But if I wait, and let a day go by, not keeping up; it will be too much and I won't be able to understand.

TIM: Okay, Dad, okay.

RUSSELL: As long as it's just a little bit, I can handle it. I can handle it. *(Exits)*

TIM: Dad?

Scene Nine

(The house. THOMAS, JANET, SANDY, *rocks.* THOMAS *is looking at* SANDY.*)*

JANET: He looks like you.

THOMAS: She looks like you.

JANET: Don't be silly. *(Pause)* I missed being quiet with you.

THOMAS: Is that why you're talking?

JANET: Talking is in my blood.

THOMAS: Talking is in only half your blood.

JANET: That's why I'm only talking half the time.

THOMAS: The awake half.

JANET: Being quiet with Polly and Russell is very loud. Even with Tim there's a big pressure to be always talking.

THOMAS: They need to know what you're thinking.

JANET: If they were quieter, they would know.

THOMAS: ...You piled the stones.

JANET: Yeah.

THOMAS: Is this going to be like being an activist? *(Pause.)* I don't know those pants.

JANET: We went shopping. I bought these. Shopping is very big. It's how people define themselves and show political allegiance.

THOMAS: *(Laughs)* I don't think so.

JANET: It is. When the citizens are displeased, they don't shop. When they don't shop, the government trembles and tries to please them, so they'll shop again. It's big.

THOMAS: Do you like shopping?

JANET: I would like it if I knew what my purchases meant. As it turns out, I bought these pants because I *like* them; they might mean something bad.

THOMAS: When I was in jail, I never thought of you shopping. I saw you giving birth, saw the airplane carrying you in the sky, remembered you giving speeches to make us radical.

JANET: Well, I was shopping.

THOMAS: Will you take me shopping?

JANET: No. We'll get an expert to take us. We won't know what our purchases mean.

THOMAS: I'm sure I won't. I don't know anything now. *(Pause. He starts to rearrange, then pile rocks.)* I used to know—when the storms were coming—where the fish were hiding. There was no *me*—I was part of everything else.

JANET: You had a big interruption. *(Helps him with rocks)*

THOMAS: It never happened before.

JANET: You never had an interruption before.

THOMAS: *(Playing)* You were an interruption.

JANET: I *tried* to be an interruption, but you turned me into a *continuation.*

THOMAS: I was very interrupted.

JANET: I'm proud to have interrupted you.

(They are happy. They pile rocks. THOMAS *stops. They listen. He hears that which was temporarily denied to him.)*

THOMAS: Oh, yes. Yes.

Scene Ten

(The house, POLLY, JANET *with* TIM*'s towel, rocks, later* RUSSELL*)*

POLLY: *(Upset)* Did you look outside?

JANET: *(Upset)* I looked everywhere. I found this. *(*TIM*'s towel)*

POLLY: What is it? Where did you find it?

JANET: Under his bed.

POLLY: *(Takes the towel)* What's on here?

JANET: Grease and dirt.

*(*RUSSELL *enters.)*

POLLY: Tim's gone. He's missing. We can't find him.

RUSSELL: What do you mean? Where's Thomas?

POLLY: He's looking outside.

RUSSELL: Did you call the police?

POLLY: The police? Did we call the police?

JANET: No, we've just been looking. The baby's gone, too.

POLLY: Oh, no! Janet, why didn't you say?

JANET: I thought as long as I didn't say, it wouldn't be true.

(RUSSELL telephones. Janet walks to the mound of rocks.)

RUSSELL: *(On the phone)* I'm at 5907 Blackhawk Drive. My ten-year-old son is missing from my house and so is the infant child of someone who is visiting me. Five, nine, zero seven, Blackhawk Drive. Please hurry. *(Hangs up.* POLLY *hands him towel)* What's this?

POLLY: It was under Tim's bed. I want to look more; I can't wait in here.

(JANET is frozen by the pile of rocks. POLLY *sees.)*

POLLY: Oh no...

JANET: I *told* him he couldn't go to the water anymore. Like Russell said.

POLLY: Show me.

RUSSELL: I'll get the car.

POLLY: No, you wait for the police, I'll go.

RUSSELL: I'll go.

POLLY: Russell, I can't just wait here; I have to go outside.

RUSSELL: All right. I ... okay.

(POLLY and JANET exit. RUSSELL *stands silently, looking around in disbelief. Then he hears* TIM*'s voice, sort of an echo.)*

TIM: Dad. Dad...

RUSSELL: Where...

TIM: I'm sorry, Dad.

RUSSELL: What is this? What's going on?

TIM: It's really tight, Dad.

RUSSELL: *(Frightened)* Ahhh... Ahhh...I...don't....

TIM: And I'm really dirty.

RUSSELL: Timmy...I'm sorry, I'm sorry, Timmy!

TIM: Dad? What's wrong?

RUSSELL: Timmy!

TIM: Dad, I'm in the wall.

RUSSELL: Ahhhhhh.

TIM: In the vent. We're stuck in the vent.

(Pause, as RUSSELL *understands.)*

RUSSELL: Tim...? Oh. Oh. *(Removes vent cover)* What are you....

*(*RUSSELL *takes baby from the vent, checks to see that she's okay, as* TIM *struggles from the vent.* TIM *reaches up for the baby,* RUSSELL *slaps his hand, is immediately sorry.* TIM *withdraws.)*

RUSSELL: Tim—

*(*SANDY *peers from the vent.)*

Scene Eleven

(The house. TIM, POLLY, SANDY, *rocks.)*

TIM: When I stand on the ground, I feel the ground all the way up myself. When I pile the stones, I feel the messages.

POLLY: What are the messages?

TIM: *(Big voice)* Don't worry when the sun goes down; it will return again tomorrow.

POLLY: *(Admonishing)* Janet says that.

TIM: Oh, yeah. I forgot. But still, there *are* messages, I just can't figure out what the words are.

POLLY: *(Slowly)* Maybe there are no words for the messages.

TIM: Yeah, that's it. There aren't any words for the messages. They're more like colors than words. Most of the messages are a deep, dark, pretty color.

POLLY: Blue?

TIM: You been getting them, too?

POLLY: Maybe. Maybe I have.

Scene Twelve

(The house. RUSSELL, TIM *and* SANDY. *Rocks)*

RUSSELL: I didn't mean to hit you.

TIM: It's okay, Dad. I did a bad thing.

RUSSELL: No, well, yes, you did do a bad thing. But that's not the point. I hit you because I was worried. And I'm sorry.

TIM: Yeah, I'm sorry, too, Dad, but you know, it's really cool in the vent.

RUSSELL: Tim—

TIM: No, it's true, Dad. The vent, it's all around you, and it hugs you, and it's little, sure; but it's also *big*, a part of something big.

RUSSELL: Tim—

TIM: Why is it so dirty?

RUSSELL: ...Well, the oil burns to heat up the air, the furnace blows the air through the vents. Some of the oil stays on the sides of the vents, so they get greasy. We didn't know it was so dirty. Men are coming to clean it out.

TIM: Who are they?

RUSSELL: Some men. Vent cleaners.

TIM: They won't hurt it, will they?

RUSSELL: They won't hurt it, what's to hurt, Tim, it's a vent.

TIM: Maybe you should call lady vent cleaners.

RUSSELL: I don't know if they have them.

TIM: They won't tear it open will they? They won't make it bleed.

RUSSELL: Nothing's going to bleed, Tim.

TIM: Because if it dies, Dad, if it dies.

RUSSELL: Tim, it's a house. It isn't going to die.

TIM: Dad, if it dies, we'll die too.

RUSSELL: Nothing's going to die. It's a vent.

TIM: It's a vent in a house on a lot—

RUSSELL: Tim—

TIM: On a street in a city in a nation on a continent on a world—

(POLLY enters with a newspaper, happy.)

POLLY: Russell, did you read about this tanker?

RUSSELL: Not another spill?

POLLY: No. It was run aground by whales.

RUSSELL: *(Disparagingly)* Is that the *Post*?

POLLY: There's photographs, Russell.

(Pause)

POLLY: Are you all right?

RUSSELL: I...I feel cold.

Scene Thirteen

(The backyard. SANDY. *Rocks.* THOMAS *and* RUSSELL *are barefoot.)*

RUSSELL: It's another way of keeping us in our place.

THOMAS: Yes.

RUSSELL: A distraction from the hellish poverty of our lives. A chance to dress up on Sunday. A chance for individual importance when we writhe in ecstacy in front of our brethren.

THOMAS: Yes.

RUSSELL: Religion is a corporate plot.

THOMAS: Um.

RUSSELL: Then why are we standing out here in our bare feet?

THOMAS: Bare feet was your idea.

RUSSELL: I am not...receptive. My shoes would get in the way of the messages, if there are messages, which I am not sure there will be.

THOMAS: We could try being quiet. Listening instead of talking. Even if you don't get a real message, there's other things that are nice—the wind, the birds, the bugs, the quiet sound from the ground.

RUSSELL: See...that...I don't.... No sound from the ground.

THOMAS: There's a sound. Maybe if you were quiet.

(A pause. The men look up.)

RUSSELL: What are those?

THOMAS: Sparrows. Those are robins. The big ones are jays.

RUSSELL: Looks like a convention. ...What are...those two?

THOMAS: ...The little one's a sparrow; the other's a jay.

RUSSELL: What are they doing?

THOMAS: *(Amazed)* ...They're...preening each other.

RUSSELL: Yes, but..they're not the same kind of birds.

THOMAS: You're right.

RUSSELL: Is that usual?

THOMAS: I've never seen it.

(A pause. RUSSELL *looks at his feet.* THOMAS *watches the birds in awe.)*

RUSSELL: *(Impatiently)* There's a parasite you can get from going barefoot.

THOMAS: I never heard of that.

RUSSELL: Yes. It burrows into your body through the bottom of your feet. Gets into the muscles.

THOMAS: Maybe you should put on your shoes.

RUSSELL: What about you?

THOMAS: I'm not worried about it.

RUSSELL: So you think you can't get a parasite because you're not worried about it? Well, that's not how it works. You can worry about it and get it, or not worry and get it. Or you can...not worry and not get it and not worry and get it.

THOMAS: Maybe we should go inside.

RUSSELL: You go.

THOMAS: Okay, Russell. Don't work too hard. *(Exits)*

RUSSELL: No words. Some non-language message. I won't recognize it if it's not language. I've dedicated my professional life to avoiding the unsaid. To not hearing the ends of incomplete sentences. "How do you do, Russell, I've heard a lot about you; I didn't know you were um, a, um." It wasn't said; it was never said. No offense was made and none was taken. Turning my back, digging into my briefcase, raising up only when I was sure the offending person's liberal facade was back in place. There was a sneer, a silent sneer every time I did *any*thing. High school? —you won't finish high school; you'll drop out. Wellll, you made it through high school, settle for that—college?! What!? Are you nuts? You won't finish *college*. Oh, you finished college—well—what? Law school?! You think you're better than everybody else? Law school? Married? You won't *stay* married? A baby? Public defenders? Hey, take the money, don't go to public defenders. So, I have a job; I have a family; I have a son; I do what I think is right, every time, and now what? It isn't enough? *(At some point he notices that he's experiencing what he is describing.)* Not enough, that's not enough? Now what? Now I'm supposed to notice the unsaid? Hear the unspoken? Pay attention to, what? Earthly body language? I'm supposed to hear a deep, pleasant sound? The sound of a million hearts beating. Supposed to notice a warm, tingling glow... Feel truth as it dances across my back... Know that I'm not alone, that I am a part, just one part...of something—big. ...Oh. Oh, yes, yes.

Scene Fourteen

(The house. THOMAS, SANDY. *Rocks. The sound of rain.* POLLY *enters with groceries.)*

POLLY: Um, hi. Where are...where is everybody?

THOMAS: They all had places to go.

POLLY: Janet?

THOMAS: Janet sometimes has places to go.

POLLY: Where—...I mean, it's your business. I'll put these away.

THOMAS: Can I help you?

POLLY: No, no. I can do it. Don't you want to go stand on the ground or something?

THOMAS: It's raining.

POLLY: Oh.

THOMAS: It's pouring, as a matter of fact.

POLLY: Yes, it's pretty relentless.

THOMAS: But I could go outside, if you want.

POLLY: Don't be silly.

THOMAS: I don't think it's silly. I think you want me to go outside, and if you do, I'd just as soon go.

POLLY: I, um. I am very sorry.

THOMAS: May I ask you a question?

POLLY: I'm embarrassed.

THOMAS: I won't embarrass you more.

POLLY: Ask.

THOMAS: Are you afraid for Russell and Tim? When I'm with them?

POLLY: Is that what you think? That I'm afraid of you?

THOMAS: It looks like that.

POLLY: *(Breath)* Well, you were wrong about your question, it did embarrass me.

THOMAS: You avoid me.

POLLY: Yes, I do, but it's not from fear. I'm not afraid of you. I don't think you're going to hurt anybody, ever again. I'm not afraid.

THOMAS: It's the best thing, to be not afraid.

POLLY: Oh, did I imply that I'm not *afraid*? I'm *afraid*; I'm deeply afraid. I'm not afraid of *you*.

THOMAS: What are you afraid of?

POLLY: I don't think I want to go into it.

THOMAS: Okay.

POLLY: *(Pause)* I'm afraid that I will be lying in bed at night and I will figure it all out—world economy, the environment, cold fusion, love, everything. And the shock of it will render me paralyzed and I won't be able to communicate. I will know how it all fits together and won't be able to share it with anybody.

THOMAS: You're afraid of losing your words.

POLLY: Got to hang on to something.

THOMAS: There aren't any words for the big things anyway.

POLLY: There certainly aren't. What's the word for how empty I feel at the shopping mall?

THOMAS: *(Playing along)* What is the word for the feeling when the sky is the right color blue?

POLLY: What is the word for I need something but I don't know what it is?

THOMAS: What is the word for feeling something bad is around the corner?

POLLY: ...Yeah. There aren't words for the big things.

THOMAS: So you shouldn't worry about losing words.

POLLY: Maybe I can't stop it.

THOMAS: I could help you.

POLLY: Don't help, please don't help. *That's* why I avoid you. It'll be just like Janet; every time Janet helps me I feel worse.

THOMAS: Why?

POLLY: Because I should have thought of it myself. You'll tell me to listen to the ground or something, and then when I do, and I hear it, I'll feel terrible because of how long I went not listening.

THOMAS: Well, I'm sorry.

POLLY: Just don't let it happen again. ...I'm kidding, hey!

THOMAS: I know you're kidding. I thought it was funny.

POLLY: Yeah, well, when that happens, you clue a person in by laughing.

THOMAS: I'll remember.

Scene Fifteen

(The house. Sound of rain. TIM *holding birdmask,* SANDY, *and rocks)*

TIM: I grew, you know.

SANDY: What makes you so sure?

TIM: That's why I got stuck in the vent.

SANDY: Ah.

TIM: People grow until they're dead.

SANDY: I thought they stopped long before then.

TIM: Nooooo. They keep growing a little, little bit. Then one day they start growing smaller.

SANDY: Then maybe you'll fit in the vents again when you're very old and small.

TIM: I don't have to go in the vents again. I'm gonna teach the baby and she can go in the vents.

SANDY: Ah.

*(*TIM *stares out window.)*

SANDY: Whacha looking at?

TIM: All the rain. Do you think it's ever gonna stop?

SANDY: It doesn't look like it.

TIM: I have to go out some time. I'm gonna give my mask away.

SANDY: You said you were going to keep it.

TIM: Yeah, but I'm not gonna.

SANDY: You going to give it to me?

TIM: Nooo.

SANDY: Who you going to give it to?

TIM: I don't know.

SANDY: How will you give other stuff away without your mask?

TIM: I don't need the mask to give stuff away. I can just give it away.

SANDY: But it might be out of order. The mask, the piles, the going away.

TIM: I don't have to wear a mask. I don't have to put it in piles. I can... put it in a bag. Just take it to a place.

SANDY: I think you're right.

TIM: I think I am, too.

SANDY: Okay. *(She starts to exit.)*

TIM: Bye. Bye bye.

(SANDY waves and exits.)

Scene Sixteen

(The house. Rain. POLLY, RUSSELL at the easel, THOMAS at the fire. Baby in cradle, easel, rocks. No SANDY. Candlelight)

RUSSELL: Did you find the batteries?

POLLY: Yes, but there's no radio.

RUSSELL: The one we took on picnics.

POLLY: Yes, Russell. Before Tim was born. I'm sure somebody in the neighborhood has a radio.

(THOMAS lights fire.)

RUSSELL: We never lit a fire in there.

THOMAS: You never needed one.

RUSSELL: Yeah, but I didn't think I'd *ever* light one because I *needed* one.

(A louder sound of rain. TIM and JANET, rain gear, enter from outside. JANET carries a piece of electrical cable.)

TIM: It's a big blackout. All of Long Island, all of New York City, half of New Jersey and Connecticut; with more cities flickering out.

RUSSELL: I finished it, Tim. Take a look.

TIM: *(At painting)* I can hardly see it.

RUSSELL: Squint.

TIM: Well, it's your first try, Dad.

RUSSELL: Not very good, is it?

TIM: It's a good first try.

RUSSELL: Maybe I need to spend more time on it.

TIM: No, just start a new one.

POLLY: What did they say on the radio?

TIM: The expressway's a parking lot.

JANET: People are leaving their cars. Downtown, too.

POLLY: They shouldn't leave their cars. Cars have headlights.

JANET: People are gathering.

TIM: They're ordering everybody to stay home.

RUSSELL: Ordering?

JANET: It sounds like ordering.

TIM: *(Big voice)* "Do not leave your homes. Repeat. Do not leave your homes."

THOMAS: Maybe we should go out. Find out why we shouldn't.

JANET: I think we should. *(She hands* RUSSELL *the cable.)* Here.

RUSSELL: What is it?

JANET: It was in the road.

RUSSELL: It looks like electrical cable.

THOMAS: Let me see. Yeah. From a power line. It's been chewed.

POLLY: Chewed?

THOMAS: These are teeth marks.

TIM: Are we going out, or are we going to do talking?

RUSSELL: We're going out. And we're going to do talking. *(He puts his arm around* TIM.*)*

POLLY: Somebody's got to stay with the baby.

JANET: She's going. *(She picks up baby from cradle.)*

THOMAS: Everybody's going.... *(To* POLLY*)* What's the word for we're all ready to go outside?

POLLY: I don't think there is one. What's the word for when I'm not frightened but ought to be?

THOMAS: What's the word for you can't be frightened when you're going outside?

POLLY: What's the word for I'm glad I'm not going alone?

JANET: What's the word for how I feel when my family is all together?

TIM: What's the word for how I feel when I'm happy?

POLLY: I think that word *is* happy, Tim.

RUSSELL: What's the word for how I feel *now,* right now?

(A deep rumble rising. They all listen. Unseen by them, SANDY *appears in full silhouette in the background. Fade)*

END OF PLAY

www.ingramcontent.com/pod-product-compliance
Lightning Source LLC
Chambersburg PA
CBHW061258110426
42742CB00012BA/1963
* 9 7 8 0 8 8 1 4 5 1 7 7 1 *